DRESS in the AGE of Elizabeth I

DRESS in the AGE of Elizabeth I

Jane Ashelford

B.T. Batsford Ltd London

First published 1988

ISBN 0 7134 5622 1

Typeset by Servis Filmsetting Ltd, Manchester
and printed in Great Britain at
The Bath Press, Avon
for the publishers
B.T. Batsford Ltd
4 Fitzhardinge Street
London W1H 0AH

Contents

ACKNOWLEDGEMENTS

I would like to thank all the private owners, museums and art galleries who provided photographs and information about the works of art included in this book, and in particular the Courtauld Institute of Art, London, for the photographs used for figures 1, 3, 4, 5, 8, 11, 12, 15, 16, 19, 20, 21, 22, 24, 25, 29, 31, 36, 38, 42, 45, 48, 52 and 98.

Introduction

'When your posterity shall see our pictures they shall think we were foolishly proud of apparell'.[1] This comment, made in 1605, reflects the single-minded interest of the Elizabethan upper classes in their appearance and their determination to make a visual record of it. They carried their seemingly unsophisticated delight in brilliant colours, luxurious fabrics and intense decorative detail to an excess which bordered on vulgar ostentation. It was not a taste which could appeal to the classically pure eye of the eighteenth century and was dismissed as 'straunge fantastick habit',[2] and 'gaudy attire'. The Victorians viewed the age in a more romantic and subjective light, their evaluation being conditioned by the endless dark and dingy portraits which peered at them through the gloom of old country houses. We are fortunate in this century to have a more enlightened attitude, being able to appreciate the full achievement of Elizabethan dress now that so many portraits have been cleaned. Once accumulated layers of dirt and varnish have been stripped, the pristine glory of the original is revealed with a freshness of colour that has hitherto been found only in Hilliard's miniatures.

Costume is the visual expression of the sensibility, preoccupations and pressures of society, and as such is an invaluable index to that society's changing attitudes. The details of costume show, to use Hamlet's words, 'the very age and body of the time, his form and pressure' (III.ii.23). The forces that moulded the costume during the period covered by this book were exceptional in English history and reflected the nation's supreme self-confidence, vitality and sheer bravado. The Elizabethans were an extrovert and extravagant people whose choice of dress and accessories was a symbol of their status and aspirations. In the strictly hierarchical society of that time it was inevitable that clothing should have been regulated by sumptuary legislation, so that it was possible to identify a man's class, rank or profession purely by his dress. This situation was changing by the end of Elizabeth's reign, much to the consternation of older and more conservative citizens who felt that values were being eroded.

The one person to whom no rules applied was, of course, Queen Elizabeth, the glittering fulcrum of England, her extraordinary jewel-laden figure becoming by the end of the reign a symbol of England's national unity and new-found power in the world. Indeed, it was thought by visiting foreigners that to have seen Elizabeth was to have seen England. This was a conscious strategy on the part of the Queen; the years 1580–1603 were extremely dangerous ones for England. The isolated Protestant island with an excommunicated Queen was under the threat of Spanish invasion and internal Catholic revolt. After the failure of the Duc d'Alençon's offer of marriage in 1582 it became obvious that Elizabeth was going to remain unmarried and that the succession problem would not be resolved until her death. The monarch, recognizing the nation's need for firm leadership and reassurance, placed herself at the focus of its attention. The portraits of her which circulated throughout England were intended not only as a reminder of her physical features but as an image 'full of glory',[3] an icon calculated to evoke in the eyes of the beholder those principles for which the Queen and her government stood.

This emphasis on appearance was a vital part of Elizabeth's strategy, for she had turned her unmarried position to advantage by encouraging the court and the country to celebrate her as Cynthia, Astrea and Diana, all goddesses famed for their chastity and purity. As it was vital that the Queen should appear to defy the normal ravages of time and retain an indestructible beauty, she relied heavily on cosmetics, using a liquid to blanch her skin and, at Christmas 1600, painting it 'in some places nearly half an inch thick'.[4] Her dress, always extravagant, was so laden with jewels and pearls that Francis Bacon suggested the Queen believed that her people, 'who are much influenced by externals, would be diverted by the glitter of her jewels, from noticing the decay of her personal attractions'.[5]

The most fashionable ladies at Court were the unmarried Maids of Honour, who were expected to provide a harmonious white, gold and silver background to reflect but not outshine the awesome figure of the Queen. The claustrophobic atmosphere at Court during the last years of the reign created many clashes between the Queen and these girls, who found their duties of attending to the bad-tempered and jealous monarch an irksome and trying experience. The impression which the Court gave to the visitor was, nevertheless, one of extreme splendour. Breuning von Buchenbach sent the following description to his master the Duke of Würtemberg in 1595: 'At no other Court have I ever seen so much splendour and such fine clothes. This holds good both of the men and of the countesses and other noble ladies, who were of rare surpassing beauty'.[6]

Under Elizabeth's influence men's dress lost the assertive shape it had acquired in her father's reign and, as it gradually became more dandified and romantic, evolved into the self-conscious elegance epitomized by the young man in Hilliard's famous miniature (fig. 40). Every aspiring courtier knew that the Queen expected him to look immaculate and fashionable at all times, so that if he was to be noticed, much effort, imagination and money would have to be spent on his appearance. In this atmosphere of intense sartorial rivalry there was a restless search for novelty, and this led to the adoption of various foreign fashions and behavioural traits. These are summed up by Rosalind in Shakespeare's play *As You Like It*, when she assesses the effect that foreign travel has had on Jacques: 'Look you lisp, and wear strange suits; disable all the benefits of your own country;

be out of love with your nativity; and almost chide God for making you that countenance you are.' (IV.i.19–33) Contemporary commentators expressed their disapproval in a variety of ways. Thomas Nashe equated the increasing volume of dress, spectacular at the time he was writing in 1593, with the wearer's increasing pride, 'They shew the swellings of their mind, in the swellings and plumpings out of theyr apparrayle.'[7]

The dramatic gestures and swaggering panache that we see in many portraits of the time are not, however, to be found in the pictures of women. On the contrary, they are depicted as pale, self-restrained creatures who stare impassively from their stiff prison of ruff, stomacher and farthingale. Perhaps this is not surprising, as the portrait was intended to be a record of the sitter's wealth and status and not a sympathetic representation of her personality. Artists were valued for their ability to record details of dress. George Gower, for example, received ten shillings for a painting of Lord Willoughby, while for Lady Willoughby, who is wearing a very elaborate costume, he received £1.[8] Gower's portraits are the culmination of an anti-realistic style in which face, figure and background interlock into one complex pattern.

The Elizabethans expressed themselves verbally and visually through allegory, that is, describing a subject under the guise of some other object of aptly suggestive resemblance. This love of complexity and ingenuity found expression in the decorative arts by the use of emblems and devices – pictorial symbols which could be incorporated into design, whether it were a costume for a tournament, an embroidered jacket, a carved fireplace or a jewelled pendant. The way in which clothes were worn, the selection of colours, accessories and embroidered pattern could convey information to an educated observer and so be a vehicle for abstract ideas. It was a language which was utilized by the Queen to convey a message of political propaganda and by lovers who could express their feelings in symbols embroidered on a handkerchief. Hence the meaning of the phrase 'printing my thoughts in lawn.'[9] Perhaps the most obvious manifestation of dress as a statement of mood was the appearance of a man in a state of melancholy, a fashionable affliction in which a disordered mind was equated with disarray in dress. When Orsino suffers from the complaint in *Twelfth Night*, the clown comments, 'Now the melancholy god protect thee; and the tailor make thy doublet of changeable taffeta, for thy mind is a very opal.' (II.iv.73)

Clothes also pleased the senses: the sense of sight through colour and pattern, the sense of smell through perfume, and the sense of touch through embellishment of surface and the combination of different fabrics. Various Italian treatises on colour and symbolism were published in England, and the extraordinary range of colours and gradations of tone which they describe are indicative of the sophisticated colour sensibility of the period. Each shade of colour had a name; shades of red, for example, ranged from the most delicate pink 'maiden's blush' to 'lustie gallant', the most vivid tone. The juxtaposition of one colour with its deeper tone was also appreciated by the Elizabethan gardener, who arranged the colours of his flowers as carefully as his own wardrobe. One such, Henry Fanshawe, did 'so precisely examine the tinctures and seasons of his flowers that in their settings, the inwardest of which that were to come up at the same time should always be a little darker than the outer and so serve them for a kind of gentle shadow.'[10]

One of the more obvious problems in studying dress of this period is the scarcity of extant garments, those that have survived being mostly embroidered jackets, gloves, coifs, stockings, partlets and forehead cloths. These represent a selection of the labours of the domestic embroiderer, who was creating ordinary garments to be worn at home and whose work does not necessarily illustrate contemporary high fashion. Of the magnificent clothes worn at the court of Elizabeth, absolutely nothing remains, but by way of compensation there are many securely dated paintings from which we can establish a fairly continuous chronology of dress. Because of practices of eighteenth and nineteenth century restorers, many paintings contain quite misleading information, the chief problems being the addition of faulty inscriptions, heavy overpainting and clumsy restoration. Added to this is the poor condition of paintings, the majority of which are oil on wood panels – a combination which is most susceptible to the damp and cold of country houses.

The literature of the period is particularly rich in references to dress and there is scarcely a play written by Shakespeare which does not allude to dress or man's revealing attitudes to it. It is rather ironic that Philip Stubbes, who inweighed against the excesses of fashion, should give in his *Anatomie of Abuses* (1583) such a detailed picture of them. Other invaluable sources are the French and Italian conversation manuals written by two Huguenot refugees who taught languages in London. Claude de Sanliens anglicized his name to Claudius Hollyband and taught the children of well-to-do tradesmen. His compatriot, Peter Erondell, taught in an aristocratic household; his book *The French Garden*, published in 1605, was dedicated to Elizabeth Barkley, the daughter of Baron Hunsdon, the Lord Chamberlain.[11] The manuals describe ordinary domestic situations in painstaking detail and so give a clear picture of what garments were worn and in what order. To these sources can be added information gleaned from private letters, inventories, official papers and wills, and so, even though physical evidence is lacking, there exists enough literary and visual material to create a lucid picture of Elizabethan dress.

To form a comprehensive picture of the relation of dress to society, one has to consider a variety of themes. Some of these have already been mentioned and will be explored in greater detail. The first two chapters, however, will trace developments in male and female dress from 1558 to 1603, elucidating wherever possible the nature of the garments mentioned in inventories and other documentary evidence and identifying them in portraits wherever this is possible.

Chapter One
Women's dress 1558-1603

THE MOST MARKED characteristic of female dress when Queen Elizabeth came to the English throne in 1558 was symmetry, with the triangular shape of the skirt in perfect balance with the inverted triangular shape of the bodice and deep hanging sleeves. Colours were sombre, and there was little embroidery or surface embellishment. Richness of effect was created by combining heavy patterned brocades, plain satins and velvets with luxuriant trimmings and linings of brown and black furs. This predominantly dark colour scheme was set off at the neck and wrists with a discreet frill of white lawn. By the end of Elizabeth's reign this sense of harmony and restraint had disappeared and the balance between bodice, skirt and sleeves had broken down, with each part of the outfit developing independently. The end result was summarized by Horace Walpole in his *Anecdotes of English Painting* as a 'vast ruff, a vaster farthingale and a bushel of pearls'.[1] It was a bizarre silhouette created by extensive stiffening and padding, and so encrusted with decoration that the natural female form entirely disappeared. Developments in fashion between 1558 and 1603 are characterized by this increasing preoccupation with decoration and exaggeration. Rapid developments in fashion were inevitable in a country whose inhabitants enjoyed a prosperous, expanding economy and a strong, stable government. Increased expenditure on clothes and a desire for imported goods transformed English fashion and led one observer to write in 1592 that English women are 'dressed out in exceedingly fine clothes, and give all their attention to their ruffs and stuffs'.[2]

Already in the 1560s colours are brighter and plain surfaces enlivened with applied decoration and jewellery (7), with puffs and slashes being employed to expose material of a contrasting colour. During the 1570s dress became highly inventive and offered women a wider range of styles and decoration to choose from. The portrait of Mary Denton (colour pl. 2) is an outstanding example of the complexity of cut and intensity of decoration available.

The period 1575–80 was a transitional one as the female silhouette became fuller and stiffer, attaining by 1585 its most harmonious appearance. The ruff had reached its greatest extent and was balanced by the wide trunk sleeves, slender bodice and bell-shaped skirt (*14*). The typical shape of the 1580s, a balance of two triangles, gave way in the following decade to a more uneasy shape with the longer and narrower inverted triangle of the stomacher extending well into the elliptical and the later rectangular shape of the wheel farthingale (*24*). The shorter skirt length and higher hairstyle gave the whole figure a rather unbalanced appearance, which was not helped by the rather shaky use of perspective displayed in most full-length portraits.

The dominant influence on European fashion during the period 1558 to 1580 was Spanish, an influence so pervasive that even the chauvinistic English could not remain immune to it. The uncompromising tenets of the Catholic Counter Reformation and the extreme formality of Philip II's court created a fashion of austere elegance that stylized the lines of the body. These severe styles and sombre colours were seen at first hand in England when, in 1554, Philip and his retinue visited England for his marriage to Mary Tudor. Their clothes impressed the English, and Spanish fashion retained a strong influence over English dress throughout the first half of Elizabeth's reign.

The distinctive shape of Spanish dress was provided by a stiff, heavily boned bodice which compressed the bust and finished in a point at the waist. This was worn with an inflexible cone-shaped skirt, the form of which was determined by an underskirt called a farthingale. The earliest mention of a farthingale occurs in the English Royal Wardrobe Accounts of 1545, when one was ordered for the Princess Elizabeth.[3] The fashion soon spread from the court to the households of the nobility and hence throughout the kingdom. The farthingale was made by stretching fabric over a series of circular hoops which increased in circumference as they descended from waist to feet. Hoops made of either whalebone, wire, rushes or wood were called 'bents', and were inserted into casings called 'ropes'. The bents gave the farthingale its distinctive shape and there are frequent references in the Great Wardrobe Accounts to their removal and renewal. Farthingales could therefore change according to fashion and there is a marked difference between the bell shape of the 1560s (*7*) and the wheel farthingale of the 1590s (*21*), which carried out the skirt at right angles from the waist to a width varying from 8 to 48 inches, before falling vertically to the ground.

English dress was indebted to Spain for its shape, but the decoration and exaggeration of certain features was unique to England. English women wore two basic garments in the sixteenth century: the kirtle, which comprised a separate bodice and skirt, and the gown. The word 'kirtle', until about 1545, denoted a garment with a square décolletage which fitted the body closely to mid-thigh and then fell in folds to the ground. After 1545, when bodice and skirt were made separately, the term 'kirtle' was applied to the skirt alone. The Spanish kirtle had an inverted V-shaped opening which was filled in with a decorative triangle of material called a forepart; this was attached to the underskirt by ties (*7, 17*). Bodice, sleeves and forepart, being detachable, were often made of the same material.

The 'round' kirtle had circular skirts which were not trained, and they were arranged so that they presented a smooth flat surface without folds, unlike the French kirtle which had stiff pleated skirts and could be worn with a forepart. Over the farthingale was worn a petticoat or underskirt, and this could be made with an attached bodice. Although an underskirt, the petticoat was usually made of a rich fabric so that it could be displayed when the upper skirt was lifted up. Those given to the Queen were particularly elaborate, as a present from Lady Paget in 1578 shows: a 'petcoate of cloth of gold and stayned black and white with a bone lace of gold and spangells layed like waves of the sea'.[4]

The bodice was referred to as a 'pair of bodys' or 'upperbodies' because it was made in two parts, the back and front being joined together at the sides. It was worn over an underbodice; this was a garment which had been stiffened by whalebone stays inserted into casings and tied there by laces or 'busk-points'. There were two basic styles of bodice. One was tight-fitting with a short point to the waist, and fastened down the side; the other had a high neck and fastened down the front. Fastening for both was usually by hooks and eyes. The neckline of the first type could either be high or low, but if the former the neckline would be filled in with jewellery, a chemise or a partlet. The smock was a fine linen undergarment worn next to the skin to protect the rich fabric of the upper garment from perspiration. It was a straight garment made from two pieces of lawn or linen about 30 to 40 inches long with a small collar, front slit or opening at the neck and long sleeves, the edges of which were usually trimmed with lace. Collar, hem and sleeve hand (the part of the sleeve nearest the hand) were usually embroidered: 'their smocks are all bewrought, about the neck and hands',[5] and in portraits this decoration can sometimes be seen above the edge of the bodice (*4, 11*). There was very little difference between the smock and the male shirt, and their similarity is satirized by Ben Jonson in *Every Man in his Humour* (1601), when a wife has to lend her husband her smock while she washes his shirt.[6]

The partlet was a decorative yoke which covered the area between the throat and the edge of the bodice and could either be made of embroidered linen, of a rich fabric studded with jewels and pearls ('their partlets set with spangs, come close up to their chinnes')[7] (*4, 7*), or of a transparent fabric such as net, cypress or fine lawn, so that the smock worn underneath it is revealed (*11*). It is often difficult to discern the difference between a partlet and a smock in a painting if both are made of the same material, and to make differentation still more difficult, after about 1560 both have a standing collar with separate ruff attached (*5*). Where partlet and sleeves were made as a matching set it is impossible to decide whether one is looking at the separate matching sleeves of the partlet or the sleeves of the smock.

It was the fashion from about 1560 onwards to have a projecting wing or padded roll on the shoulder, the purpose of which was to hide the ties which united sleeve and bodice. The wing grew in size as the fashion developed, and it became a decorative feature which could be slashed to show puffs of the smock underneath, decorated with aglets or adorned with bows (*7, 8, 9*).

A top garment which was worn either for warmth or on formal occasions was the gown. In the first 40 years of the sixteenth century the gown was worn over the kirtle. It was a voluminous garment with a square neckline which fitted the body closely to the waist and then fell in ample folds which, until 1530, were usually trained. In about 1550 two different styles began to emerge – the loose, which was usually made in one piece, and the closed, in which the skirt would be attached to the upper part. The closed gown fitted to the waist (*3*) and then extended over the hips to fall in heavy folds to the ground. Its collar could either be small and turned down, or high-standing. There were a variety of closed gowns – the 'Dutch' or round gown which did not have a train, the 'Flanders' which had a fitted bodice and stiff collar and the 'Italian' which had a double bodice. The loose gown was also called open ('call my taylor to bring my gowne, not the close one but my open gowne of white satten layed on with buttons of pearle'[8]). It fitted the shoulders (*2*) and then fell in set folds which spread outwards to the ground, leaving an inverted V-shaped opening in front from neck to hem. If required the gown could be closed from neck to hem by means of buttons, bows and aglets.

The observation in Tomkis's play *Lingua* that a 'ship is sooner rigged than a gentlewoman made ready'[9] is pertinent when one considers the amount of time involved in placing so many garments on the body, the intricate task of pinning and tying them together, the arrangement of the lady's hair and the application of cosmetics. In one dialogue in *The French Garden*,[10] Lady Ri-Mellaine is getting dressed. After the maid has warmed her smock, she puts it on; on top of it is placed the bodice of her petticoat, which in turn is laced into place, to be followed by the petticoat skirt and stockings, secured by garters. The maid then tightly ties her 'Spanish leather shoes', these shoes being chosen because lady Ri-Mellaine wants to go out for a walk. The next task is to arrange the lady's hair and so a cloth is placed over her shoulders while her hair is combed thoroughly. The maid is told to bring some jewels to decorate the hair and some 'laces to bind my haires'. At this point in the proceedings paste of almond is brought so that Lady Ri-Mellaine can wash her face; a piece of scarlet cloth is used as a flannel and her face is dried with a napkin. Then a carcenet is arranged round her neck and agate bracelets round her wrists and the tailor is ordered to bring an open gown and farthingale. The next part of getting dressed is a tricky one – the selection and fixing of neckwear. A cutwork rebato (a shaped collar wired to stand up round the back of the head) is chosen and pinned to the bodice (presumably the bodice of the gown), and the cuffs are secured with 'small pinnes'. Finally gown and farthingale are arranged and a girdle is placed round the waist. A selection of useful accessories includes a comfit-box, mask, fan, handkerchief, gloves and a chain of pearls.

Fig. 1 shows a portrait of 1550–55, thought to depict Elizabeth, Countess of Shrewsbury, wearing a loose gown. It has two vertical bands of embroidery down the front and corresponding bands on the puff sleeves and sides. A soft white fur lining is visible down the centre, where it is fastened at regular intervals by aglets. The fur is also revealed through aglet-decorated slits on the short upper sleeves and sides, and it forms a neat collar. The undersleeves have a geometric pattern of interlaced circles and this design is also visible on the partlet which is worn close round the neck under a thick rope of pearls. The ruff is here still in embryonic form as a frill attached to the smock. It was made by gathering a band of fine linen, the edges of which had been embroidered with coloured silks or black-

1. Elizabeth, Countess of Shrewsbury (?), Follower of Hans Ewörth, 1550–55, (The National Trust, Hardwick Hall)

A REGINA

2. Brass rubbing of Philipe Bedingfield, wife of T. Darcy, 1559. (By courtesy of the Board of Trustees of the Victoria & Albert Museum)

work. The hair, neatly parted in the middle, is worn with a French hood, that is, a small hood worn on the back of the head with the crown raised on a horseshoe-shaped wire over the head. A brass rubbing dated 1559 (*2*) gives a clear idea of the appearance of the loose gown. In this fairly plain example the front ties are loosened to let the material fall in heavy folds to the ground.

By 1559 the ruff had become an accessory in its own right and its closely pleated and decorated layers rose up and framed the wearer's face. In the 1560s the detached ruff was starched and usually worn with the tasselled strings (bandstrings) that drew it together either left dangling or pushed out of sight. A portrait of an unknown woman dated 1560 (*3*) shows the embroidered ruff nestling round her face with a matching ruff at the wrist. The flamboyant undersleeves are a striking feature of her outfit, arranged so that tight bands of embroidery alternate with puffed sections slashed to show the underlying smock. Her closed gown is close-fitting and enlivened with panels of darker fur arranged in a herringbone pattern. Pairs of aglets are arranged down the front of the gown, round the collar and on the short puff sleeves. The pronounced heart-shaped curve of her hood suggests that it is a Mary Stuart hood, a style thought to have been introduced by Mary Stuart that eventually superseded the French hood. The French hood, however, remained a favourite with older ladies for many decades.

As the 1560s progressed, the surface of the gown became more broken up by decoration and the contrast between its dark surface and the black and white patterns on sleeves and ruffs more marked. This move towards a more ornamental style becomes apparent when one compares this portrait of Eliza-

3. *Unknown lady. Hans Eworth, 1560,* (Private collection)

A. 1567.
ÆTA, SVÆ
. 18.

beth, Countess of Shrewsbury (*1*) with a portrait of Elizabeth (?) Boleyn dated 1567 (*4*). The latter's gown is also lined with white fur, but it has a deep V-shaped opening with wide fur revers that form a luxurious collar and is further decorated with tasselled braid and looped-up chains. The

4. Elizabeth (?) Boleyn. Unknown artist, 1567. (The Trustees of Birr Castle Estate, courtesy of the Earl and Countess of Rosse)

5. Mary (?) Boleyn. Unknown artist, 1567. (The Trustees of Birr Castle Estate, courtesy of the Earl and Countess of Rosse)

oversleeves of the gown have been cut into sections each one of which displays its white fur lining, and the undersleeves have a large-scale embroidered pattern of flowers as has the edge of the smock which is visible beneath the partlet. Delicate chains are strung across the area between

6. Mildred Coke, Lady Burghley. Unknown artist, c.1566. (By courtesy of the Marquess of Sailsbury)

the embroidered ruff and the edges of the partlet and smock. The decorative appearance of the embroidered caul (a closely fitting hairnet) speckled with spangles confirms a poet's description of 'calles of golde beset with spangs'.[11]

Mary (?) Boleyn, sister of Elizabeth, wears a similar outfit (*5*), but without a gown, so disclosing her lavishly embroidered partlet and matching sleeves, but in this portrait the smock is not visible. Like her sister, she has chosen to wear a caul made from the same material as the partlet, and has placed a flower that could be either a marigold or a daisy behind her ear. The pins that attach her chain to the front of the bodice are clearly visible.

A portrait of Mildred Coke in 1565 (*6*), the wife of William Cecil, Lord Burghley, illustrates the next stage in the gown's development. Mildred was 37 when this portrait was painted and so advanced in her pregnancy that her girdle swells out over her stomach. She gave birth to Robert, who eventually succeeded his father as Elizabeth's principal adviser. The loose gown of rich figured velvet, studded with jewelled quatrefoils, is not fastened together and has hanging sleeves, a curved stand-up collar and scalloped wings. Under it is worn a black bodice enlivened with wavy lines of gold braid and a black brocade skirt. A partlet with matching sleeves is embroidered with a delicate pattern of interlocking ovals, with a central flower motif composed of pearls. In one hand she holds a bunch of cherries and in the other a pomander.

7. Unknown lady. Attr. Steven van der Meulen, 1567. (Yale Centre for British Art, Paul Mellon Collection)

The typical style of bodice and skirt worn in the 1560s can be seen in a portrait of an unknown girl painted by Steven van der Meulen in 1567 (*7*). The bodice narrows in a straight line to a point below the waist, whereas the skirt swells out with close-set pleats like a bell and is parted to show a smoooth, plain underskirt. Vertical bands of embroidery enclosed within braid further accentuate the gradual lengthening of the bodice, and zig-zag lines of the same embroidery alternate with irregularly placed puffs on the sleeves. The main decoration on the outfit are pearls – single pearls are placed down the centre of the bodice and round the neckline, and edge the opening of the gown. A matching caul and partlet are encrusted with smaller pearls arranged in a latticework pattern, and the edge of the smock is visible under the partlet. Jewelled ropes consisting of clusters of pearls and beads are draped across the bodice and partlet, and a large very ornate jewel is pinned to the centre of the bodice. A similar rope of pearls and beads is used as a girdle. Three strings of a much smaller and more delicate pearl necklace are worn under a closed ruff; the hand ruffs match this.

8. Lady Bacon, terracotta and polychromy, c. 1567. (Private collection)

A terracotta bust of Lady Bacon, *c.*1565 (*8*), demonstrates an alternative and simpler way of decorating the bodice. The borders of the centre fastening and edges of the wings have been cut up so that they form a series of interlocking tabs. This method of decoration, equally popular in male dress, was called 'pickadil'. The surface of the bodice and sleeves has been 'pinked': the tiny cuts are arranged in neat vertical rows with three larger cuts arranged diagonally. The standing collar of the smock, topped with a closely gathered ruff, is clearly visible, as is the way in which the French hood is wired to grip against the sides of the face.

In the Tate Gallery in London is a splendid portrait of an unknown lady (possibly a Wentworth) painted by Hans Eworth between 1565 and 1568 (colour pl. 1.). The dramatic decoration on her closed black gown consists of bands of gold metallic embroidery, clusters of pearls and rubies and bands of looped metallic braid. The wings, from which fall narrow hanging sleeves, are accentuated by a band of embroidery that curves round the shoulder seam. Her matching red and gold brocade sleeves and underskirt are covered by a latticework pattern of pearls. An elegant

9. Anne Russell, Countess of Warwick. English school, 1569. (By kind permission of the Marquess of Tavistock, and the Trustees of the Bedford Estates)

Anne

black velvet court bonnet with an ostrich feather trim rests on top of a caul that matches the sleeves. Her jewellery is particularly impressive: the pendant suspended from her girdle depicts a goddess dressed *in antica forma*, the mirror held in her hand juts out of the frame. Twisted round her neck are thick ropes of pearls, interspersed with gold beads, from which hangs a pendant of ruby, jet and pearl.

The desire for more variety of decoration is also apparent, but less opulent, in the portrait of the Countess of Warwick, *c.*1569 (*9*), in which the gown is embellished with aglets and a chain of pearls secured with a bunch of fresh flowers on the breast. Wearing fresh flowers was a common practice in the summertime and was a habit that irritated the moralist Stubbes: 'And in the summertime while flowers be greene and fragrant . . . they will carye in their hands nosegayes and posies of flowers to smell at; and which is more 2 or 3 nosegayes sticked in their brests befor, for which cause I cannot tel, except it be to allure their Paramours to catch at them.'[12] Striped gauze oversleeves are worn with the embroidered undersleeves.

The late 1560s saw a much brighter and fresher palette of colours and one of the most popular combinations, red, black, white and gold, can be found in the portrait of Lady Kytson painted by George Gower in 1573 (*10*). The vivid red of the sleeveless gown is set off by its wide black fur collar and red, black and white braid trimmings, but the striking foliate embroidered design on the sleeves is softened by gauze oversleeves. A gathered gauze partlet discloses a delicate necklace of tiny black beads and the edge of an embroidered smock. Lady Kytson appears to be dressed for outdoors as she is wearing and not carrying her gloves; furthermore she has donned her hat with a tall crown, jewelled hatband and white ostrich feather over a linen under-cap.

In the same year that the likeness of Mary Kytson was made, Mary Denton sat for her wedding portrait (see colour pl. 2). Her father, Sir Roger Martyn, was a mercer who became Lord Mayor of London in 1567. It is thought to be a wedding portrait because her wedding ring is displayed on her left hand and the lozenge of arms in the background includes those of her husband's parents.[13] Her complex outfit consists of a black damask overgown which has turned-back revers with a patterned lace edging. The edges of the revers are decorated with spangles, and the left-hand one stands up sharply to form a high collar. The overgown curves into the waist and appears to be attached to the bodice; the sleeves have been cut away to reveal a full undersleeve decorated with the same lace as the revers and the partlet. In addition to the dramatic twisting shape produced by these two layers, the top sleeve is further cut up and decorated with strips of gold braid and gems. No longer a flat yoke, the partlet is gathered into folds which form at the top a ruched layer under the ruff. Under the gown is a dull red velvet bodice covered in small white bows, gold chains and embroidery; it matches the overskirt, which has been pulled up to disclose a white underskirt. Lace ruff and hand ruffs are decorated with gold spangles. This proliferation of applied decoration – embroidery, narrow strips of braid, bows, spangles and lace – is a sign of fashion's increased preoccupation with pattern and avoidance of plain surfaces.

10. Elizabeth Cornwallis, Lady Kytson. George Gower, 1573. (The Tate Gallery, London)

ANº DNI 1573
ætatis suæ 26
LADY KYTSON

11. Catherine Parr. Unknown artist, 1576. (The National Trust, Coughton Court)

A portrait entitled 'Catherine Parr' and dated 1576 (*11*) shows a further extension of the upstanding collar as it provides increased width across the shoulders. The embroidered pattern of strawberry plants on the collar is repeated on the gauze partlet, beneath which the top of the embroidered smock is clearly visible.

At about this time it was the fashion to wear a ribbon across the bodice from which was suspended a piece of jewellery. The one worn by Catherine Parr is fairly simple and serves to accentuate the width from one edge of the collar to the other. A rather more elaborate version appears in a portrait of Lady Knollys of 1577 (*12*), where one loop of twisted braid is threaded through a jewelled parrot, and a further chain of pearls comes across the right shoulder to be attached to the jewel and then disappears at the left side.

The period 1575 to 1580 was a transitional

12. Lady Knollys. Attr. Clouet, 1577. (Present location unknown)

ANº DNI 1577
E K

13. Dame Philippa Coningsby. English school, 1578. (Indianapolis Museum of Art, James E. Roberts Fund)

one as the female silhouette became fuller and stiffer. A comparison between the unknown girl of 1567 (*7*) and a portrait of Dame Coningsby painted in 1578 (*13*) shows the extent of that progression. The elegant tapered lines of the earlier costume have been replaced by a more swollen and rounded shape which is accentuated by a tiny waist, while the wings are less prominent and used only to carry into the sloping line of the very full sleeves. The increased width of the neckline causes the partlet to become a continuous piece of material through which can be seen the three embroidered edges of the smock. The head is now separated from the body, as the ruff has deepened and thickened and there is a corresponding change in the shape of the hand ruff. The arrangement of chains and the yellow ribbon across the bodice and partlet are similar, but the jewellery has become more delicate in design. An increased desire for width can also be seen in the shape of the hair; it is now puffed out on both sides of the head and the jewel-encrusted bonnet that adorns the head is flatter and longer so that it balances the wider shape.

It is apparent in the portrait of Mary Cornwallis of *c.*1580–85 (*14*) that the new shape has now fully developed. The square neckline has disappeared and the bodice has become longer and narrower, curving into a pearl-decorated point which rests on the skirt. The wings on the shoulder have shrunk and have ceased to be a decorative feature, while the enormous swollen sleeves, embroidered with a large-scale blackwork pattern, now serve as the focal point of the outfit. Gauze oversleeves are worn with them, and both sleeves are finished with a blackwork frill. The degree of increased width and the enlargement of pattern on the sleeves can be gauged when this sleeve is compared with Lady Kytson's of the previous decade. The skirt is cut to show a brocade underskirt which has an intricate interlaced design with flowers within each compartment. The ruff, in a figure-of-eight shape, is slightly tilted and

14. Mary Cornwallis. George Gower, c.*1580–5.* (Manchester City Art Galleries)

15. Susan Jermyn. Circle of Gower, c.1585–90. (The Lord Tollemache, Helmingham Hall)

has widened and deepened to such an extent that it encroaches on the face, causing the pearl ornaments on the caul to rest on it. The looped-up chains that were such a distinctive feature of the 1570s are replaced by thick ropes of pearls which would remain fashionable until the end of the Elizabethan period. Two jewels are pinned to the bodice, and a jewelled miniature hangs on a white silk ribbon attached to the girdle. From this point the bodice and skirt have the appearance of one inverted triangle intersecting another, their straight lines emphasized by the triangular shape of the stomacher and forepart. The enormous width of hem is balanced by the width across the arms.

The pose of Mary Cornwallis, one hand slipped through a rope of pearls and the other holding a feather fan, seems to have been a standard one in the 1580s and can also be seen in a portrait of Susan Jermyn (*15*) and one of Queen Elizabeth (*16*). Susan Jermyn wears a striking outfit dominated by sleeves ornamented with lines of white puffs which alternate with large white flowers with red sequin-studded centres. Puffs form a strong vertical line down the centre of the bodice. A smooth rich grey and ochre brocade forepart is worn with the skirt, its sophisticated pattern contrasting with the simple stylized shapes of the

16. Queen Elizabeth I. English school, c.1585–90. (The Abbot and Community of Ampleforth Abbey)

17. Lady in court dress. Nicholas Hilliard, c.1580–5. (By courtesy of the Board of Trustees of the Victoria & Albert Museum, London)

flowers. The lawn figure-of-eight ruff is extremely wide and is tilted at a greater angle than that worn by Lady Cornwallis. In the rather harsh portrait of Queen Elizabeth at Ampleforth Abbey the pose draws attention to the Queen's magnificent rope of pearls and her long, slender fingers. A number of portraits of the Queen from this period depict her wearing a circular cutwork rebato that curves round the back of her head like a halo. It is an effect that is accentuated by the radiating pleats of the head-rail.

The full-length silhouette typical of the mid-1580s can be seen in a drawing, attributed to Hilliard, of a court lady (*17*). The Spanish farthingale skirt has attained its greatest width and after this date is replaced by the wheel or French farthingale. The six bows down each side of the skirt are doubtless there to attach the forepart to the remainder of the skirt, for the detachable

18. Elizabeth Brydges. Hieronimo Custodis, 1589. (By kind permission of the Marquess of Tavistock and the Trustees of the Bedford Estates)

ÆTATIS SVÆ, 14
ANNO DNI, 1589
Elizabeth Bruges daughter to the Lord Giles Chandos

forepart allowed the wearer to change her colour schemes at will. A miniature is suspended from a bow on the lowest point of the bodice.

Elizabeth Brydges, the daughter of Lord and Lady Chandos, painted by Custodis in 1589 (*18*), wears an open cutwork ruff which is pinned to each side of the bodice. It was usual practice for unmarried girls to wear open ruffs. The area disclosed by the ruff is filled in with a delicate pearl necklace and the blackwork-embroidered edges of her smock are clearly visible above the curved line of the bodice. Turned-back cuffs are embroidered in a similiar way and are edged with gold lace and spangles, but the matching grey and black brocade bodice and skirt has softer lines and a less exaggerated shape than the costume worn by her mother (*69*). Elizabeth wears a quantity of jewels; an opal in a gold setting is secured to the right sleeve by a pink ribbon, a gold, ruby and jet jewel is pinned to the other, and thin gold chains are looped across the bodice and pinned at its centre with a red bow and a jewelled pot of flowers. Another jewel adorns her ruff and three more are pinned to her hair, which is brushed smoothly off the forehead into two puffed-out and rounded shapes.

An alternative style to the bodice and skirt ensemble can be seen in a 1590 portrait

19. Amy Gurdon. Unknown artist, 1590. (Private collection)

20. *Lady Mary Sidney. Attr. Nicholas Hilliard, c.1590.* (Private collection)

of Amy Gurdon (*19*), who wears a smock embroidered in blackwork with a pattern of oak leaves, vines and carnations. It is worn under a closed gown which has been tied round the waist with a ribbon. The gown sleeves, edged with gold braid, have been cut away to reveal the smock, and braid also borders the revers and skirt of the gown. Thick looped chains had become rather unfashionable by this date.

Amy Gurdon's costume is relatively comfortable when compared with the clothes worn at court (*21, 98*). Lady Mary Sidney, sister of Sir Philip Sidney, was at the centre of a glittering circle at court and her choice of neckwear for a miniature portrait by Nicholas Hilliard, *c.*1590 (*20*), demonstrates the extreme style that would be considered fashionable by her circle. Her elaborate cutwork ruff would have required hours of preparation to starch and pleat. Even more time would be needed to arrange it to stand at such an acute angle. A shadow of matching cutwork rests on her softly curled hair, in which have been placed sprigs of honeysuckle. The simplicity of the headdress contrasts with the formality of the neckwear – presumably a deliberate effect.

Mary Kytson, daughter of Lady Kytson (*10*), married the Earl of Rivers in 1583; details of the material and trimmings purchased for the trousseau are discussed in Chapter 3. Her portrait was painted by an unknown provincial artist, possibly Hubbard, in 1593, when she was 24 (colour pl. 3). The marriage was not going well at the time the portrait was painted, and by 1594 she had separated from her husband for good. The Countess's sleeveless loose gown, stomacher and exaggerated sleeves are embroidered with a dramatic pattern of hops and carnations in gold and black. The white stomacher has a strong central line of gold braid and is further decorated across the top with five heavy gold gems. Attached to a red ribbon round the right sleeve is a pendant. A red skirt with five silver braid guards and a silver fringe is worn over a wheel farthingale. An interesting feature of the outfit is the gauze apron with its delicate lace edging and embroidery. The fashion for wearing elaborate, decorative aprons (see also *52*) was criticized by Gosson in 1596:

> These aprons white of finest thread
> So choicely tied, so dearly bought,
> So finely fringed, so nicely spread,
> So quaintlie cut, so richly wrought'.[14]

The black loose gown with hanging sleeves is richly embroidered in gold with a design of honeysuckle, so forming an effective frame to the brilliant red, gold and silver colour scheme of the rest of the outfit. Even her pet dog has a colour co-ordinated ribbon leash.

A magnificent set of four portraits by the same unknown artist, belonging to the period 1590 to 1600, are in the collection of the Viscount Cowdray at Cowdray Park (one of the set, a portrait of Lady Elizabeth Southwell, is discussed in Chapter 6). Another, entitled 'Queen Elizabeth' (*21*), *c.*1595, is a splendid example of the new fashion for wearing a bodice and skirt of different embroidered patterns. Here the white satin bodice and sleeves are embroidered in brilliant colours with a strikingly naturalistic design of flowers and fruits, the stems encircling these motifs being decorated with pearls. The white satin skirt worn over the wheel farthingale is covered with a profusion of pearl-studded embroidery, with the main motifs being a pyramid interspersed with the interlaced stems of vine leaves, fruits, knots and snakes. The pose, one hand resting on the edge of the farthingale, is a typical one at this time, as the skirt could extend from the waist for a distance of up to 48 inches. (Indeed, the greatest desire of one 14-year-old girl in 1597 was 'to have a French farthingale laid low before and high behind and broad on either side so I may laye mine arms on it'.)[15] The open ruff is powdered with jewelled brooches representing arrows made of red and gold enamel set with rubies; the feathers are made of pearl. These spiky shapes are echoed by the seven jewelled points finished in pearl that adorn her head.

Figures 22 and 23 provide an interesting sidelight on the main role of women in sixteenth-century society, that is, the producing and rearing of children. The first portrait is of Alice who married Sir Julius Caesar in 1595 and bore him three sons. Her portrait was painted in 1597 (*22*), when she was 31 years old and pregnant. Her fashionable outfit has been modified so that the rigid understructure can accommodate her swollen stomach. The high value placed on the creation of a family and the concern that posterity should be aware of the family's achievement meant that it was considered quite normal to have a portrait painted when the wife was in a state of advanced pregnancy. We know from the diary of Arthur Throckmorton that in 1587 he paid the artist Hubbard £7 for his wife's portrait. Four days later she gave birth to a girl; the child died the following month. In March 1588 she again sat for her portrait, and this time the artist was Jeronimo (probably Hieronimo Custodis) and the payment was

21. Queen Elizabeth I. Marcus Gheeraerts, c.1595. (By kind permission of the Viscount Cowdray)

22. Lady Alice Caesar. Unknown artist, 1597. (C. Cottrell-Dormer)

£4. She was pregnant again and went into labour two months later, but as there is no further mention of the child it must have died or been stillborn.[16]

The second portrait, of an unknown lady and her nine-month-old child, is dated 1598 and is now in the Rhode Island School of Art and Design, Providence, USA (*23*). The mother's highly fashionable outfit has one distinctive feature: the partlet has been turned back on one side to display her breast. Whether this is an indication that she is suckling the child it is difficult to say,

23. Unknown mother and child. English school, 1598. (Museum of Art, Rhode Island School of Design, Providence, Rhode Island, U.S.A)

Æ·SVÆ·24·
Æ·9·MONT

24. Grace Wilbraham. English school, 1602. (The Lord Tollemache, Helmingham Hall)

but it seems unlikely that a lady of her station would not be using the services of a wet nurse. The embroidery on her stomacher and partlet is a good illustration of the rather heavy and emphatic style prevalent at the close of the century. Many writers were concerned that the stomacher, with its whalebone busks and stiffening, could impair a woman's child-bearing potential;

> . . . the baudie buske that keepes down flat,
> The bed wherein the babe should breed.[17]

Needless to say, their warnings were ignored and the stomacher by-passed the waist and extended well into the farthingale skirt by the late 1590s.

Francis Bacon's observation that 'There is no excellent beauty that hath not some strangeness in the proportion' is particularly true of the female silhouette of the late

25. Anne Conningsby. Attr. Gheeraerts, 1603. (By courtesy of the Earl of Wemyss and March)

daughter of
Conningsby
to Anne of
of James
parried to Sir Rich
The figures
stand for 1603
the ancient way
lating the

Elizabethan and early Jacobean period.[18] The bodice remained elongated whilst the hem shortened and the general impression that this created, with the bodice set square on the tip-tilted flounced farthingale, was that the outfit was a size too small for the wearer. This final stage in Elizabethan fashion can clearly be seen in the portrait of Lady Wilbraham, dated 1602 (*24*). The wings have again become a distinctive feature as they project out over the shoulder, giving the illusion of narrowing the top of the bodice. This is long and pointed, and has a deep border of overlapping tabs which rest on the sloping line of the skirt. Lady Wilbraham wears an open figure-of-eight ruff and her hair is dressed in a simple bouffant style trimmed with puffs of feathers. An inscription on the portrait of Anne Conningsby (*25*) shows that she was a Maid of Honour to Queen Anne of Denmark and that the portrait was painted in the year of King James's accession to the throne, 1603, so it is likely that Anne is wearing her court costume. Again, the most prominent feature of her costume are the huge sequin-decorated wings and the tabbed border round the ludicrously exaggerated stomacher. The delicate, wired pearl headdress is a variant of the type worn by Elizabeth's Maids of Honour (*98, 99*).

Chapter Two

Men's dress 1558-1603

MEN'S DRESS AT the time of Queen Elizabeth's accession in 1558 was generally restrained and dignified, epitomized by rich, dark colours set off at neck and wrists by white frills, enlivened by gold embroidery, slashing and a profuse use of aglets. The clothes followed the lines of the body fairly closely, and, apart from the shape of the trunk hose, with little exaggeration of any one feature. This was in complete contrast to the style that emerged in the 1580s, when male dress attained its most extreme and artificial shape. A ruff encircled the head, effectively isolating it from the body, a padded doublet curved into a point below the waist, the hose were minimal and the thighs were encased in tightly fitting canions. It was a combination which demanded a well-proportioned figure and long, shapely legs. The emphasis on an elongated, tapering waist, wide circular ruff and swollen hips and arms was common to both sexes and was indicative of the move towards a less aggressively masculine style. These taut, tense lines did, however, in the next decade, give way to a more relaxed and romantic style as the doublet became looser and was worn undone. A soft lawn falling collar replaced the ruff and the hair was worn longer and arranged in natural-looking curls. It was a change in mood that coincided with the flowering of English sonnet writing at a court which was dedicated to praise of the virtues and beauty of its ageing Queen. Poets and artists alike pretended that time had stood still and that the Queen's beauty remained undimmed:

> Times young howres attend her still,
> And her Eyes and Cheekes do fill,
> With fresh youth and beautie;
> All her louers olde do growe,
> But their hartes they do not so,
> In their Loue and duty'.[1]

Elizabethan society evaluated an individual's status by his or her appearance, and this emphasis on the benefits of the public display of dress are summarized by Ben Jonson in his play *Every Man Out of His Humour*:

> Rich apparel has strange virtues; it makes him that hath it without means esteemed for an excellent wit; he that enjoys it with means puts the world in remembrance of his means: it helps the deformities of nature, and gives lustre to her beauties; makes continual holyday where it shines; sets the wits of ladies at work, that otherwise would be idle; furnisheth your two-shilling ordinary; takes possession of your stage at your new play. (II.iv.42–8)

The court was the perfect stage for the man who wanted public acclaim for his finery, but he would have to be a wealthy man indeed to sustain a stay at court for over a week. Many changes of wardrobe would be required, and any lessening in the quality of the outfits and any repetition would soon be noticed and commented on. The remark in *Every Man Out of His Humour* is probably no exaggeration; 'twere good you turned four or five hundred acres of your best land into two or three trunks of apparel'. (I.ii.36)

Many writers deplored the fact that men would squander the revenues of their estates in this way, and an instance of this is recorded by Arthur Throckmorton in his *Diary*. When he went to Court in 1583 (his sister married Sir Walter Raleigh), he financed his new clothes by selling part of his land and by borrowing his brother's legacy, on which he paid interest for many years. Laurence Stone's paper, *The anatomny of the Elizabethan aristocracy*, examined the huge debts accumulated by the aristocracy during the last years of Elizabeth's reign and concluded that one of the essential components of this display of 'conspicuous consumption' was an extravagance in dress.[2] Stone cites the case of the Earl of Arundel, who owed £1,023 to 42 mercers, silkmen, tailors, embroiderers and other tradesmen. The Earl of Essex owed his draper £736 and the Earl of Leicester owned seven doublets and two cloaks valued at £543. This was an extraordinarily high sum, in view of J. Black's estimation that the value of plate in a nobleman's establishment (the most expensive part of the household goods) ranged in value from £1,000 to £2,000 or of the fact that the cost of the entire winter uniform for an officer serving in Ireland in 1599 totalled £4 0s. 10d.[3]

Another less exclusive but equally effective way to 'publish your clothes' was available in London in the middle aisle of St Paul's Church, where the gallants would strut up and down in their new clothes between 10 and 12 o'clock in the morning. Since their intention was to impress all present, the tailors, hiding behind the pillars, would treat the occasion as an impromptu fashion show and make notes on the latest cut, colour, trimmings and accessories. Thomas Dekker, in *The Guls' Horne-Booke* advises that '4 turns' in the Walk were sufficient, as a fifth would mean that your outfit 'would be stale to the whole spectators'.[4]

Motivated by this desire for ostentatious display, the fashionable Englishman would insist on fashions that were 'farre-fetched and deare bought',[5] and flitted excitedly and indiscrimately from one foreign style to another adding to them glittering surface decoration. It was a source of great annoyance to contemporary writers that their fellow countrymen not only adopted but exaggerated foreign fashions. George Gascoigne commented on the irony that we can 'mocke and scoffe at all contryes for theyr defects' and yet we 'doo not onlye reteyne them, but do so farre exceede them: that of a Spanish Codpeece we make an English football; of an Italyan wast, an English petycoate, of a French ruffe, an English chytterling.'[6] As early as 1554 when Philip II of Spain visited England, the strong vertical lines and severe colour schemes worn by the Spanish had influenced fashion. From the French were borrowed the long cloak, the cartwheel ruff, the peascod doublet, brief trunk hose, pantofles, curled hair and a variety of effeminate accessories, blending with a myriad of other ideas from the Low Countries into a unique style.

When the fashionable man got dressed in the morning he required the help of a servant to sort out and air his clothes. Once they were placed on his body in a satisfactory manner, the servant would tie them together, a process that was both time-consuming and fiddly. The 'uprising in the morning' is the subject of a dialogue in Hollyband's *The French Scholemaister*, Eliot's *Parlement of Prattlers* and Florio's *Second Frutes*.[7] From these sources we gather that the servant's first task was to warm his master's shirt; he then found out what type of neckwear he required that morning and warmed it in front of the fire after checking that it was clean and the bandstrings were in place. Once the shirt and neckwear had been arranged, the master decided what 'suit' (matching doublet and hose) to wear, and it was duly fetched out of the clothes chest and thoroughly brushed. The sequence of garments worn on a cold day was first shirt, then waistcoat, then doublet and finally jerkin. Doublet and hose were then united by threading the points through the eyelet holes round the waistline of both garments and then tying them securely together. A girdle would be placed round the waistline and to it would be attached a dagger and a rapier. Netherstocks (stockings) would be pulled on over the legs and secured with a garter. Choice of footwear depended on the weather; in the *Parlement of Prattlers* there is a choice between pumps and pantofles, single, double and three-soled shoes. A gown or cloak was then placed over the whole ensemble, a hat placed on the head, and the servant's final task was to check that his master had a pair of gloves, lined if the day was cold, and a clean handkerchief.

The shirt (*26*), a straight linen garment, was usually embroidered round the neck

26. Man's embroidered shirt, c.1588. (The Museum of Costume, Bath)

opening, standing collar and sleeve hand. Until the 1580s the only visible areas of the shirt were the standing collar and wrist ruffle, but if it was worn with a slashed doublet, an embroidered section could be pulled through the slash (*30*). Embroidered shirts could be very expensive if bought ready-made. Henry Percy, 9th Earl of Northumberland, paid £7 5s. for one in 1586,[8] so Stubbe's complaint in 1583 that shirts covered in 'needleworke of silk and curiouslie stitched with open seame and many other knackes beseydes' could cost '10 shillings, some 20, some 40, some £5, . . . and some £10',[9] does not appear to be exaggerated.

A collar of Holland cloth, lawn, or cambric worn around the neck of a shirt was known as a band. The ruff developed from a frill edging at the top of the standing collar of the shirt. It slowly increased in size until it became a separate article that could be starched and goffered. The small ruff, whether separate or attached to the shirt, was usually worn open in the front during the 1560s, and the tasselled ties (bandstrings) which unite it are clearly visible in portraits of this date (*30, 31*). When the closed ruff was worn the strings were pulled together, tied and then concealed (*36*). The pleats or 'sets' of the male ruff were made in the same way as the female ruff, that is, by placing wet, starched fabric over a hot 'poking' or setting stick. The falling band, or fall, was a collar which rose from the upper edge of the shirt neckband and was worn over the collar of the doublet, but it did not become a separate article until the mid 1580s, when it was left open at the throat (*39, 45*).

Ruffs attained their maximum complexity and size in the late Elizabethan period and were arranged in double, treble or more layers which formed either a horizontal figure of eight or massed convolutions in several layers (*46, 47*): 'labyrinthinian set, whose thousand double turnings never met'.[10] These elaborate starched ruffs completely collapsed when it rained, much to the delight of Stubbes who felt this was an apt punishment for those men foolish enough to use the 'devil's liquore'; 'they goe flip flap in the winde, like rags flying abroad, and lye upon their shoulders like the dishcloute of a slut'.[11]

A young man who wished to be thought fashionable might well need to 'lie ten nights awake, carving the fashion of a new doublet'[12] for there was an enormous variety in the shape, trimming and sleeve design of doublets. Two to four yards of material were required for the outside of the garment; then there was the lining and decoration of either lace and embroidery, or panes, slashing or pinking. All these methods of cutting the surface of the doublet were intended to show the colour of the lining so that there was a rich contrast of colour and texture. Fastidious Brisk's description of an assault made on his doublet in *Every Man Out of His Humour* gives some idea of how elaborate this could be: 'He (making a reverse blow) . . . strikes off a skirt of a thick-laced satin doublet I had lined with some four taffetas, cuts off two panes embroidered with pearl, rends through the drawings-out of tissue, enters the linings, and skips the flesh.' (IV.vi.101–6)

Fastening could be by buttons, hooks and eyes, lacing or ties down the centre. The doublet fitted closely and was shaped to the waistline and pointed in front so that as the waistline curved downwards the point became sharper and deeper, until in about 1575 the point was padded to such an extent that it overhung the girdle (*42*). The resulting shape, called a peascod, was created by stiffening the front of the doublet with pasteboard or busks and heavy padding at the point of the waist. The padding was called bombast, and could be made from horsehair, flocks, rags, cotton, flax, rags and even bran. According to Stubbes, this created a number of problems for the wearers, who could 'hardly eyther stoupe downe, or decline them selues to the grounde, soe styffe and sturdy they stand about them'.[13] Another prominent feature of the doublet was the standing collar, which during the period 1560–70, reached its maximum height almost to the ears (*31*) and was often topped with pickadils – stiffened tabs joined and turned out at right angles (*32*).

Over the doublet was worn a jerkin (*34, 88*). This was a sleeved or sleeveless lined garment whose shape was dictated by the style of the doublet. It was not worn open and would be fastened down the centre with buttons, hooks and eyes, lacing or points. Jerkins also gave scope to the embroiderer's skill. The Earl of Rutland paid his embroiderer the huge sum of £60 for a 'jerkin and paynes of heare coulour velvet, all embroidered with flames of gold and silver'.[14] It was common practice to perfume jerkins, and in Ben Jonson's play *Cynthia's Revels*, 1601, the perfumer assures a customer that the perfume he has used for his jerkin is 'pure benjamin, the only spirited scent, that ever awakened a Neopolitan nostril. You would wish yourself all nose, for the love on't' (V.iv.309–11). The leather jerkin, a military garment adapted for civilian use, was also known as the buff jerkin, as it was made of buff, an ox-hide dressed with oil. This type of jerkin, a relatively inexpensive garment, went out of fashion in the mid 1570s, but remained in general use during the seventeenth century.

A padded garment which could be worn under the doublet for warmth or worn as an informal top garment was the waistcoat, and there is a reference to its use as a warm undergarment in Florio's *Second Frutes*, 1591, when a master asks for his waistcoat and his servant replies:

> Which wilt you have that of flanell?
> —No, give that which is knit.

When the waistcoat was worn informally it was usually richly embroidered and could be bought ready-made in a milliner's shop by the end of the century. In Jonson's play *Cynthia's Revels*, 1601, one of the characters wears a 'rich wrought waistcoat to entertain his visitants in, with a cap almost suitable' (II.i.33–4).

The variety of styles and decoration available for doublets was matched only by the variety of styles in the hose, a situation that was the subject of much contemporary satirical comment from dramatists, pamphleteers and other observers of the contemporary scene: 'Let me see what breeches wore I a Satterday? let me see: a Tuesday, my Calymanka; a Wednesday my peach collor satin; a Thursday my Vellure; a Friday my Calymanka againe, a Satterday let me see my riding breeches.'[15] Hose consisted of two parts: upper or trunk hose, also known as breeches, and lower or nether hose, which could either be canions (from the 1580s onwards), or stockings; thus the term 'hose' can refer to either part. Before 1570 the upper hose and stockings were usually sewn together to form a single garment, but after that date they were increasingly worn as separate articles united by garters or points. The most popular form of upper hose was, by 1558, trunk hose, and until the 1570s the most fashionable style was called 'Spanish Kettledrum';

this style reached to mid-thigh and was distinguished by a round onion-like shape achieved by stuffing (*27*). The style that succeeded it sloped outwards from a small waist to a maximum swelling below and then turned directly on to the thigh (*33*). It was usual to make both types of hose in panes, strips of material which parted slightly to disclose a rich lining (*27, 28, 33*), and, as with doublets, the combination could be very rich. By the 1580s the full rounded trunk hose had shrunk to a mere pad round the hips worn with canions (*42*). Canions were close-fitting extensions from the trunk hose to the knee which required one and a half to two yards of material and were always lined. They could be of material that contrasted in colour and fabric with the upper hose (*45*), or could be made as a matching set (*46*). Separate stockings were worn with canions and could either be pulled up above the knees or fastened over the canions with garters.

Stockings could either be made from material cut on the cross, or be knitted. Silk stockings imported from Italy were the most highly prized and expensive, but the price of silk stockings was generally high (between 7 and 40 shillings) and this drove many gallants to dye their stockings if the original colour went out of fashion. Hosiers sold a range of stockings from cloth and worsted (the finest came from the Channel Islands) to silk. In Florio's *Second Frutes* (1591)[16] the servant is instructed to: 'Goe to my hosier . . . and bid him bringe me tomorrowe morning 5 or 6 payres of silk stockings of the very best, of sundrie colours, and as many of the best worsted hosen that he hath.

When very fine stockings were worn with boots they were protected from possible damage by boothose, and although the boothose was essentially a protective garment, it also became very ornamental. 'They haue also bootehose which are to be wondered at . . . they must be wrought all over, from the gartering place upward, with nedle worke, clogged with silk of all colors, with birds, foules, beasts and antiques purtrayed all ouer in comlie sort'.[17] No wonder, then, that this accessory could cost up to £10.

27. Prince Alexander Farnese. Alonzo Coello, c.1560. (The National Gallery of Ireland, Dublin)

Breeches were an alternative form of hose and were fuller and longer. They were available in three basic styles, venetians (*34, 35, 48*), galligaskins and open. Stubbes observed that galligaskins were 'long and wide, reaching down to their knees onely with three or four guards apiece laid down along either hose'.[18] All baggy breeches that were closed at the knee were known as 'slops' or 'slop hosen'.

One of the most prized items in the fashionable man's wardrobe was a cloak, so Sir Walter Raleigh's reputed action of throwing his over a puddle would have been considered an act of supreme sacrifice. Fashions in cloaks changed with bewildering swiftness, a situation summed up by the ever-observant Stubbes:

> Cloakes of dyverse and sundry colors, white, red, tawnie, black, greene, yellowe, russet, purple, violet, and infynite other colours: some of cloth, silk, velvet, taffetie and such like, whereof some be of the Spanish, French and Dutch fashion. These cloakes must be garded, laced and thorowly faced; and sometimes so lyned as the inner side standeth almost in as much as the outer side; some have sleeves, other some have none; some have hoodes to pull over the head, some have none; some are hanged with points and tassels of gold, silver or silk, some without al this'.[19]

The way that a man wore his cloak

depended on which national style he preferred, for he could choose between the Spanish, French and Dutch fashion. The Spanish cloak was hooded, very full and short, while the Dutch was hoodless, heavily guarded and worn with the wide sleeves hanging loose (*38*). The French cloak (*42, 44*) was generally worn over the left shoulder, and although it was fastened under the arm it was very difficult to keep on. This short cloak was displaced in the 1580s by the long French cloak that reached to the knees or ankles and was again thrown over one shoulder. Needless to say, cloaks could be extremely expensive, for they had a 'store of workmanship bestowed upon them'.

There were quite a large choice of outer garments available if something more substantial than a cloak was required. One such was the cassock, a loose hip-length garment widening towards the hem. It had a narrow standing collar and full sleeves which were either elbow-length or wrist-length. A plain undecorated cassock was popular with the middle classes and during cold weather it was often worn for warmth when travelling. It could also be a very elaborate garment; the Lord Chamberlain's accounts contain references to cassocks of crimson velvet embroidered with gold, trimmed with lace and lined with crimson sarcenet. Another garment was the coat, a lined garment which fitted at the waistline and reached to the knees. The mandilion was a loose hip-length jacket with a standing collar and hanging sleeves. The side seams were open, producing a front and back panel, and it was buttoned from collar to chest only and put on over the head. Robert Sidney, in a portrait in the National Portrait Gallery (*41*) wears his mandilion 'Colley-Westonward', a title which derives from a Cheshire saying for something going wrong. The garment is worn sideways with the front and back panels draping the shoulders, one sleeve hanging down in front and the other behind.

Ankle-length gowns were worn by academics, men of the legal profession, doctors, civic and Crown officers, and on ceremonial occasions. As the length of the gown reflected the dignity of the wearer's profession, the gowns of working men were restricted to calf length, except for men who were over 60. In such cases the gown would be worn over doublet and jerkin, and was made with a fitted yoke from which ample folds of material fell to the ankles (between 6 and 12 yards were required for the gown). Until around 1570 it was fashionable to wear a gown open in front to the knee and unconfined by a girdle, but after that date the ankle-length gown seems to have been worn without a belt or girdle. Gowns were frequently lined and guarded with fur, and the type of fur chosen would be a reflection of the wearer's status. In Florio's *Second Frutes* (1591) there is a list of the contents of a gentleman's wardrobe and it includes four gowns: a long gown furred with marten, a gown lined with an unnamed fur, a night-gown of chamlet and a gown lined with rug (a hairy or shagged frieze).

An essential part of the fashionable man's outfit was a hat with a richly decorated band and feather plume. The number and variations of styles in hats are too many to enumerate, with crowns ranging from high to flat and brims from narrow to wide. The materials used included silk, velvet, taffeta, sarcenet, felt and leather. Beaver hats were very fashionable and expensive, such as the one which excites the admiration of Amorphus in Jonson's *Cynthia's Revels* (1601):

> AMORPHUS: Good faith, this hat hath possest mine eye exceedingly; 'tis so pretty and fantastic: What? is it a beaver?
> ASOTUS: Ay sir, I'll assure you 'tis a beaver, it cost me eight crowns but this morning.
> AMORPHUS: After your French account . . . A very pretty fashion, (believe me), and a most novel kind of trim: your band is conceited too.
> (I.iv.147–56)

It was important that the hatband should be unusual and highly decorated (*54*). The most popular material was cypress (a silky fabric), made with a cable twist and finished with a bow. The hatbands of the very wealthy were sometimes made either of jewels or pearls or both – one composed entirely of pearls and valued at £30 was stolen from Sir Walter Raleigh's house in 1584.[20] Jewels could also be pinned to the hatband (*38, 42*). Feather shops supplied the fashionable man with ostrich feathers of all colours for his hat. They could be worn either as a single plume, in a bunch, or with another feather such as osprey or heron. Whichever feather was favoured, it was often encrusted with spangles, but if the wearer was caught in a shower of rain the splendid effect was lost. The enormous sums of money that were spent on clothes can be gauged from the fact that one imported ostrich feather, even before it went on sale in the shop, represented the approximate equivalent of a labourer's pay for five days' work.[21]

Gloves were another vital accessory. They seem to have been made with gauntlets only after about 1590, but both styles were cut so that there was little variation in the length of the fingers. The gauntlet section was decorated with embroidery (*74*) and trimmed with braid and fringing, any embroidery being first worked on satin, cut out and then sewn on. Perfumed or 'washed' gloves were first imported from France and Spain, but after 1580 were being made in England. When Rowland Whyte went on a shopping spree for his employer, Sir Robert Sidney, in 1595, he assured him that he would

> sett in hand all these parfumed gloves you wryte for, which shall be hastened unto you. And will seeke all over Cheapside for shag and taffeta answerable to this a pattern you send me.

Four weeks later he wrote:

> I doe send your lordship foure paire of flaneld gloves, six paire of plaine gloves: two paire of shagd gloves trim'd with gold and silver lace, two paire of gloves lined through with vellat, there was no shag to be found neare the pattern and therefore I have ventured to send these, but they will be changed againe if they serve not your turn.[22]

Presumably as it was winter, Sidney required gloves that were both elegant and warm.

There were four basic types of footwear available to the Elizabethan man; slippers, pumps, shoes and boots. The lowest-cut items of footwear, covering only a part of the foot, were known by the generic term of slippers; those covering all the foot but having a single sole were called pumps; those covering the foot to the ankle were termed shoes; and those extending to the calf or knee were boots. Footwear had a general tendency during the period towards a narrower, bluntly pointed toe and a gradual increase in the thickness of the sole. Pantofles had long front uppers only, and were worn indoors as slippers and outdoors as an overshoe. Their soles were made of cork which thickened towards the heel, the height of the sole becoming more exaggerated by the end of the century. The uppers could be pinked, embroidered and trimmed with metal lace and spangles. Stubbes could not understand why a man should want to

HASARD
FORDVARD
GEORGE LORD SETONE

wear such a highly decorated and essentially unpractical style of footwear outdoors, for pantofles would be very difficult to keep on and 'with their flipping and flapping up and downe in the dirte they exaggerate a mountain of mire, and gather a heape of clay and baggage together'.[23]

The Duke of Mantua observed in 1557 that men were wearing either the short Spanish cloak or the long fur-lined gown that was so popular in the previous reign.[24] Typically Spanish dress of the period can be seen in Coello's portrait of Prince Alexander Farnese (*27*). He wears a dull gold cloak of brocade with its characteristic pomegranate pattern. The cloak has been casually slung across the shoulders as if it were a cape and is lined with ermine, a fur reserved for the nobility. A matching doublet decorated with lines of braid is fastened down the front with pearl buttons, the high collar being matched by a similiar one on the cloak. The beginnings of the ruff are discernible in the neckband, which like the wristbands, is pleated. Through the gold embroidered panes in his hose the lining is clearly visible, and the sleeves are alternating bands of slashed white satin and gold embroidered satin. The whole effect is one of sumptuous elegance achieved by perfect cut and by using the richest fabric which needs no further ornamentation.

A 'suit', that is, a jerkin worn with matching doublet, hose and cloak, can be seen in this portrait of George, 5th Lord Seton (*28*). He was Controller of the Household of Mary, Queen of Scots, a position made plain by his rod of office inscribed with Mary's cypher and the pattern of embroidered thistles on red velvet. The most striking feature of his outfit is the very high standing collar attached to his short cloak and its correspondingly wide revers. The paned trunk hose are squareish in shape and the codpiece is clearly visible. His flat-crowned bonnet has a crown as wide as the very narrow brim and from the right side droops a spangle decorated feather.

28. George, 5th Lord Seton. Unknown artist, c.1557. (National Galleries of Scotland)

29. Unknown man. Hans Eworth, 1560. (Private collection)

In a portrait by Eworth of an unknown gentleman, dated 1560 (*29*), we can see that the ruff has developed into a more decorative accessory. Resting on the pickadil border of his doublet collar, it is embroidered with blackwork and forms at its edge

Edwd De Vere
7th El of Oxford

30. Edward de Vere, 17th Earl of Oxford. English school, c.1565. (By courtesy of Christie's)

a vertical figure of eight. His doublet is fastened down the front with gold buttons (the shank and attachment of the first one can be clearly seen) and its surface is adorned with vertical lines of braid in between which are bands of small slashes. A black velvet-collared cloak is worn across the shoulders. This rather restrained outfit is augmented by one piece of jewellery, a thick rope of linked chains very similar to those worn by women, which remained a popular accessory for both sexes throughout the decade.

The decoration on Sir Richard Knight-

31. Sir Richard Knightley. Unknown artist, 1567. (By kind permission of the Firle Place Trustees)

32. Anthony Browne, Viscount Montague. Attr. Hans Eworth, 1569. (The National Portrait Gallery, London)

ley's costume of 1567 (*31*) is restrained but elegant, with its small precise black and white pattern arranged in neat vertical lines. Knightley wears a doublet that has a curved shape, high standing collar and narrow pickadil hem. The top button is left undone, as is the ruff, so that the bandstrings are left to hang loose. A contrasting pattern decorates the paned trunk hose, worn with the codpiece. (The codpiece, during the reigns of Henry VIII and Edward VI, was the visible expression of man's virility and much attention was drawn to it. With the decline of aggressively masculine fashion it was not felt necessary for it to be such a focal point, and so it gradually disappeared from male dress.) A correspondingly high collar is attached to the sleeveless fur gown worn over the doublet and hose. The locket which hangs on a ribbon round Knightley's neck probably contains a miniature.

A change of mood was introduced by the new decade, for the 1570s brought in lighter, brighter colours, a greater originality and variety of cut, and a more marked use of braids, pinking and embroidery. This change can be observed by comparing Eworth's portrait of Viscount Montague in 1569 (*32*) with that of Sir Philip Sidney (*33*) in 1577. The most marked difference is the more pronounced peascod shape and narrower skirt of the doublet, the fuller, more swollen style of trunk hose and the deeper, closed ruff. Decoration on Viscount Montague's costume is restrained and limited to plain lines of embroidery on the doublet and four pairs of aglets on the sleeves of the gown. Gold embroidered panes on Sidney's trunk hose are much more flamboyant, and

33. Sir Philip Sidney. English school, c.1577. (The National Portrait Gallery, London)

the surface of the white leather doublet has been broken up by vertical slashes and pinking. The metal gorget worn over the doublet was the prerogative of military men, who were allowed to wear it with civilian dress.

In the same year, 1577, Martin Frobisher had his portrait painted by Cornelius Ketel (*34*). It is an informative portrait from the point of view of dress, as it shows the

34. Sir Martin Frobisher. Cornelius Ketel, 1577. (The Bodleian Library, Oxford)

method of fastening the hose to the doublet. He wears voluminous venetians with looped borders in pickadil at the knees, the jerkin, shirt and wings being decorated in the same way. His jerkin is tied by points but is open lower down, disclosing doublet and stray points which fasten the breeches to the underside surface of the doublet. The fullness which is apparent in the venetians is echoed in the modified trunk sleeves of the doublet.

An alternative style of venetians is worn by the future James I in a portrait dated 1574 (*35*). His green velvet pear-shaped venetians are closed beneath the knees with a pickadil border and are worn with a cream-coloured doublet and closed ruff. His bonnet has a high crown and a bunch of pink, green and white ostrich feathers. Pickadil decoration has also been applied to the double wings of the jerkin, a sign of the increased attention given to this part of male dress.

The closed ruff of the 1570s is recorded in meticulous detail in a portrait of Philip Howard, 1st Earl of Arundel (*36*). The edge of the fine linen ruff has been cut into a series of alternate lines of small slashes, circles and triangles, and then trimmed with bobbin lace. The bandstrings have been tightly drawn in so that the close-set pleats encircle the head.

The interest in applied decoration that developed during the 1570s is matched by a quest for more vivid and striking colour schemes, an example being the costume worn by the Earl of Leicester in a series of portraits executed during the late 1570s. He was a man whose intense love of finery earned him a respected position as arbiter of taste among the fashionable men at Elizabeth's court, and it is a reputation which is borne out by a portrait, painted

35. James VI.
Attr. Rowland Lockey, 1574.
(National Portrait Gallery, London)

A°·Æ·18

36. Philip Howard, 1st Earl of Arundel. Unknown artist, 1575. (Reproduced by permission of His Grace the Duke of Norfolk)

around 1577 (colour pl. 5). He wears a salmon-pink doublet with matching sleeves, which has been slashed and pinked in a neat diagonal pattern. It buttons up the front and has the same slight peascod shape as that worn by Sir Philip Sidney (*33*). A high-standing collar edged in pickadil supports a lace-edged ruff and the narrow skirts of the doublet and doublet wings are treated in the same way. The embroidered panes of the hose are now set wider apart so that they disclose their rich brocade lining. The codpiece has almost disappeared. Instead of the chunky jewellery of the previous decade a finer, more elegant chain from which is suspended the Lesser George of the Order of the Garter is worn round the neck. A bonnet with jewelled hatband and feather is worn at a slight angle.

All the garments worn by Leicester became the subject of exaggeration during the next two decades, but, as illustrated in this portrait, they are in a state of balance, with the volume equally distributed between doublet and hose. After this date each garment develops independently and the balance breaks down as the doublet belly swells out and under into the curious peascod shape and the hose shrink to a mere pad round the hips. Leicester's ruff, so carefully contained above the standing collar, is destined to extend far beyond it so that the head is effectively disconnected from the body. Decoration, whether pinking, slashing, braid, lace or embroidery, becomes similarly more prolific as the garments increase in volume. Leicester's costume represents a successful integration of the English preference for surface decoration with the Spanish taste for severity of

37. Sir Jerome Bowes. Unknown artist, c.1584. (Suffolk Collection, Ranger's House, Blackheath)

cut, a style which made an impact by its elegance and richness of material. In the next two decades the search for novelty, whether home-grown or imported, was to lead to a series of fashion excesses which would give the Elizabethan period its unrivalled reputation for extravagant flamboyance.

The last thing that an Elizabethan man wanted to do with his cloak was to wear it the way it was designed to be worn. Sir Jerome Bowes, an impressive man reputed to be 'three storeys high', was sent by

38. Sir Henry Unton. Unknown artist, 1586. (Reproduced by permission of His Grace the Duke of Norfolk)

Elizabeth in 1583 to be her ambassador at the court of Ivan the Terrible of Russia, and during his eventful stay there Bowes impressed the court with his tenacity and toughness. His portrait was painted shortly after his return to England in 1584 (*37*). The preference in the 1580s for cloaks with definite patterns of vertical or diagonal stripes of gold braid against a dark background can be seen in Bowes's short bottle-green cloak, liberally decorated with gold braid and worn with the sleeves hanging loose. His white and gold paned trunk hose are worn with gold and white brocade canions. White stockings are secured with garters fringed with gold and the doublet is ornamented with regular lines of gold braid and horizontal lines of very narrow slashes with long gold chains looped across. A falling band is turned down over the doublet with its two edges overlapping, but after 1585 the falling band is worn with a considerable gap between its edges.

The immense width attained by the ruff during the 1580s is well demonstrated in a portrait of Sir Henry Unton (*38*), painted in 1586 when he was Elizabeth's ambassador to the Low Countries. He wears a Dutch cloak in the fashionable manner, draped over one shoulder. It is lavishly guarded with gold braid and has large ornamental buttons. The plaited red and white braid which secures it has been threaded through the doublet to emerge on the right shoulder where it is tied in a bow. His tall-crowned hat is trimmed with a cypress hatband and an ostrich feather topped with an osprey feather and a large jewel.

Two noblemen, Sir Walter Raleigh and an unknown man who might be the Earl of Essex, wore the height of fashion when their portraits were painted in 1588 (*39, 40*). Certain elements of their outfits, cloaks slung nonchalantly over one shoulder, curly hair, peascod doublets and brief trunk hose, are borrowed from French fashion and indicate the Englishman's eclectic attitude to dress during the 80s and 90s. Raleigh's cloak is very dramatic with its deep fur collar and alternating straight and wavy lines of seed pearls, ending in a trefoil of three large pearls. A love of surface

39. Sir Walter Raleigh. Attr. 'H', 1588. (The National Portrait Gallery, London)

40. Unknown man, Nicholas Hilliard, c.1588. (By courtesy of the Board of Trustees of the Victoria & Albert Museum, London)

decoration can be seen in the treatment of their doublets. The peascod doublet worn by the unknown man is composed of interlocking panels of serrated black and white material, while Raleigh's has been cut up all over to produce an uneven surface, so creating interesting variations of light and shade. Both garments are fastened down the centre with large ornamental buttons. Raleigh's love of pearls is aptly illustrated in this outfit, for large pearls form the buttons, two are worn as earrings, a pearl bracelet is worn round the wrist, and embroidered seed pearls cover the hose and cloak.

The trunk hose worn by both men, although diminutive, are still cut into panes which are themselves embellished, and the brevity of the hose leaves the white stocking-clad legs fully visible. The unknown man has chosen to wear a cartwheel ruff, while Raleigh wears four transparent

41. Robert Sydney, 1st Earl of Leicester. Unknown artist, c.1588. (The National Portrait Gallery, London)

1591
THOMAS CANDYSH
BY MARK GERARDS

42. Thomas Cavendish. Unknown artist, 1591. (By permission of the Trustee of the Will of the 8th Earl of Berkeley, deceased)

lawn collars placed on top of each other, a popular fashion, as this quotation from Thomas Dekker's play *The Honest Whore* (1604) makes plain:

> I wouldst thou give me five yards of Lawne to make my punke some falling bands a the fashion, three falling one upon another; for that's the new edition now. (III.i.142)

Another style of ruff is worn by Henry Herbert, 2nd Earl of Pembroke, when he had his portrait painted in about 1590 (see colour pl. 6). It is multi-layered in the shape of a flattened figure of eight and arranged so that it rises up at the back. A courtier's comment in the anonymous play *The Old Law* that his doublet needed 'three hours a buttoning' (IV.i.160) does not perhaps seem so exaggerated when we look at the Earl's pinked, peascod-bodied one. Over it is worn an unbuttoned brown jerkin with vertical lines of gold braid. The rather cumbersome shape of the paned trunk hose, with bands of heavy metallic embroidery, contrasts with the skin-tight canions. Pembroke, being a Knight of the Garter, signifies this by wearing the Lesser George round his neck, and the Garter insignia encircles his coat-of-arms.

By the early 1590s the peascod doublet had reached absurd proportions, typically shown in a portrait of Thomas Cavendish (*42*), where the belly of the doublet is so exaggerated that it has curved back upon itself and his hose are even briefer than those worn by the unknown man of fig. 40. Cavendish, like Raleigh, was particularly fond of pearls. His doublet is embroidered with seed pearls in a pattern of drooping flowers, the panes of the hose are encrusted

43. Unknown man. English school, c.1590. (Present location unknown)

with pearls, and he appears to be wearing canions embroidered in the same way as the doublet. His cloak, worn on one shoulder, has been thrown back to display elaborate pearl-embroidered fastenings, and a plain falling band is worn under a transparent one. He holds a tall-crowned hat to which is pinned a large osprey feather jewel with one large pearl suspended from it. Another pearl is worn as an earring.

An even more effeminate appearance is presented by an unknown young man of about 1590 (*43*). Two of the most reviled male fashions that originated in France were the use of feather fans and make-up, 'when a plumed fan may shade thy chalk'd face' (1597).[25] Both are in evidence in this portrait. The subject stands in a picturesque bower of eglantine and honeysuckle wearing a peascod doublet embroidered with an extravagant large-scale design of flowers. The doublet is fastened with enormous buttons and covered with transparent gauze. The French influence was so pervasive that a visitor to the English court in 1592 observed that 'the lords and pages of the royal court have a stately, noble air, but dress more after the French fashion, only that they wear short cloaks, and sometimes Spanish caps, and not such broad hats as the French'.[26] A woodcut of a fashionable Frenchman from Jean de Glen's *Des habits, moeurs, ceremonies . . . du monde*, 1601, (*44*) illustrates the briefness of their trunk hose and the very short cloak, though this was soon replaced by a longer one.

44. French gentleman. From Jean de Glen's Des Habits . . . du monde, *1601.* (Courtesy of the Trustees of the British Museum)

During the 1590s there was a tendency towards a more relaxed, softer and less rigid look, seen in a portrait of Charles Blount (*45*). He wears his lace-decorated jerkin buttoned halfway down and across its revers is spread a delicate lace falling band. His hose are cut much squarer than before and worn with contrasting brocade canions. The full-length version of this style can be found in Gheeraert's portrait of the Earl of Essex painted after his return from Cadiz in 1596 (*46*). His matching doublet, hose and canions are made from a silvery-white spotted satin, closely fitting but not restrictive. The skirts of the doublet are now in evidence again and, in both cases have been cut at an angle. Decoration in Essex's suit is restrained and limited to vertical lines of narrow braid. The paned

45. Sir Charles Blount. Unknown artist, 1590–3. (By permission of the Trustees of the Mapledurham Collection)

ÆTATIS SVÆ 24
S^R CHARLS BLVNT K^T THERD SONNE O
S^R MICHEL BLVNT OF MAPELDERHA
IN THE COVTY OF OX

PENSE
Robert Earle of Essex
Lord Deputy of Ireland

46. Robert Devereux, 2nd Earl of Essex. Attr. Marcus Gheeraerts, c.1596. (By kind permission of the Marquess of Tavistock and the Trustees of the Bedford Estates)

silver hose are similiar to those worn by Blount.

The garments chosen by Sir Walter Raleigh for a portrait of 1599 (*47*) again display his great love of pearls: the already heavily embroidered jerkin and paned hose are further encrusted with pearls. Unlike the portrait of ten years earlier (*39*), the doublet is no longer distended by stuffing and is far less exaggerated in shape. The silk scarf tied round his arm could be a

47. Sir Walter Raleigh. English school, 1598. (The National Gallery of Ireland, Dublin)

48. Sir Reginald and Lady Mohun. Unknown artist, 1603. (By permission of Lord Dunraven, Adare)

lady's favour, as it was usual for the military to wear a scarf draped across the body and tied under the arm: 'What fashion will you wear the garland of? About your neck like an usurer's chain or under your arm like a lieutenant's scarf?'[27]

The less rigid and more comfortable styles that developed during the Jacobean period are hinted at in a portrait of Sir Reginald and Lady Mohun, of about 1603–5 (*48*). His extremely full gathered breeches reach to below the knee where they are fastened with a fringed bow, and the doublet, like the breeches, has a tiny spot pattern and is fastened down the centre with a row of very small buttons. A wide falling band rests on the doublet and jerkin with a very deep edge of lace. Above the small closed ruff is a falling band, an instance of a fashion that continued until about 1615. Over the doublet a jerkin with extended wings is worn open and decorated with interlocking lines of braid, the skirts being divided into square overlapping tabs. Rich embroidery on the sword belt and hangers is typical of this period. The Earl of Northampton, for example, had a 'girdle and a pair of hangers of nedle worke of silver and golde and silke and full of strawberries and powdred with pearle, lined with tawney velvett', valued at twenty shillings.[28] Sir Reginalds's shoes have flat heels and are fastened with a bow over the tongue.

The gradual deflation of the male silhouette that had occurred at the end of Elizabeth's reign continued throughout the Jacobean period. The earlier exaggerated fashions that had accentuated individual parts of the body were discarded in favour of a more unified and graceful look and with the more general use of the falling band the head was no longer visually isolated from the body. The functional purpose of incidental items of dress such as sashes and shoe roses was hidden as they became focal points of decoration and were smothered in spangle-encrusted lace and ribbon.

Chapter Three

'The mart of fools': London and the fashion trade

A VISITOR TO London in 1599 remarked that 'This city of London is so vast and nobly built, so populous and excellent in crafts and merchant citizens, and so prosperous, that it is not only the first city in the whole realm of England, but is esteemed one of the most famous in the whole of Christendom'.[1] Unprecedented economic expansion and a period of peaceful, stable government had led to increased expenditure on dress and a desire for imported goods. London was an international marketplace for the luxury textile trade and the mercers of Cheapside had an unrivalled reputation for the quality and range of their silks, brocades and velvets. The fashionable man or woman who required ready-made garments and accessories, whether it be a waistcoat or a spangled feather, would be able to find what they wanted in the 'Pawn', the shopping area situated on the south side of the Royal Exchange. This prestigious building, erected by Sir Thomas Gresham and completed in 1570, was a hive of commercial activity and a fashionable meeting-place. Specialists in the fashion trade were located in specific areas of the city, so that an area became synonymous with a particular trade, for example, Budge Row with furriers and Silver Street with wigmakers.

Foreigners were always impressed by the quality of clothes worn by the citizens of London and by the frequent and often outrageous changes in fashion. One, Emanuel van Meteren, in 1575, was prompted to write: 'The English dress in elegant, light and costly garments, but they are very inconstant and desirous of novelties, changing their fashions every year to the astonishment of many'.[2] It is apparent from contemporary references that there was a considerable interchange of visual information between England and the Continent and that this is how information about new fashions was disseminated. In Lyly's play *Midas*, 1592, there is the comment that the tailor has 'gone to the painters to learn how much more cunning may lurk in the fashion that can be expressed in the making'.[3] That tailors consulted paintings and drawings for ideas is confirmed by Ben Jonson in *The Staple of News*, published in 1625 and acted in 1609:

> I pray thee tell me, Fashioner, what authors
> Thou read'st to help thy invention? Italian prints?
> Or Arras hangings? They are tailors' libraries.
> (I.i.101–3)

It also seems likely that fashion dolls were circulating in England, for it was a method of passing on information that was used as early as 1396 at the French court, when records show that a tailor was paid for making a doll's wardrobe. A direct reference to the existence of fashion dolls in England occurs during the trial in November 1615 of Mrs Turner, who was tried as the accomplice of Frances Howard, Countess of Somerset, in the murder of Sir Thomas Overbury. Among the exhibits were clothed and naked models of men and women and when they were shown in court an eyewitness said: 'I was present at their arraignments and the pictures, puppets and magic spells were no other but several French babies, some naked, some clothed, which were usual then, and so are nowadays, to teach us the fashions for dress of ladies' tiring and apparel'.[4] Fashion dolls were probably handed down to children when they had served their purpose, and a likely example of this use can be seen in a 1577 portrait of Arabella Stuart, aged 23 months, which depicts her holding a very sophisticated doll wearing a highly detailed costume of the mid 1560s (*49*).

Ordering a complete set of new clothes was not a regular occurrence and would be reserved for a special occasion like a wedding. If the family were wealthy and wanted the display to be impressive the cost involved was great. When Mary Kytson (see colour pl. 3) married Lord Darcy in 1583, her parents spent £203 5s. on 'divers parcells of silke' for the 'apparellynge of her for her marriage'. The rest of the trousseau was equally lavish, with £48 10s. 8d being spent

49. Arabella Stuart. Unknown artist, 1577. (The National Trust, Hardwick Hall)

on ruffs, sleeves and partlets; 6 embroidered smocks and 4 embroidered cauls were bought for £18 0s. 18d, black velvet to line a nightgown cost 40s. 3d, 2 pairs of silk hose £4 and silver and gold lace £31 15s. 10d. It cost £14 14s. 3d to have these garments made up.[5] It is not surprising that her family commissioned the fashionable artist George Gower to paint a marriage portrait of her that year,[6] for her appearance represented a considerable financial investment on their part.

Mary would have taken the silk along to a tailor and described the style she wanted. He would then cut it by taking a pattern from one of her existing gowns. The tailor charged for the labour involved in making the required garment and any extra material that had to be purchased (usually lining, trimmings and fastenings). That this method was not always foolproof is shown by this letter from the son of a Shrewsbury tailor to Sir William Langley in 1594:

> for the other gowness yo'r measures were so ill taken that the tailor sayes he cannot tell what to make of them but we will take the best course with the advice of Elin Stanley, with such lace as shall be requist – for the cloak and safeguard, it shall be made ready. I will buy the cloth of such colour as the tailor shall best advise me, and will see it set forward against the time of your letter for the french bodyes and furdinall sleeves; I think there be not any in our town being so small, but if not, we will get them made so soone as I can.[7]

Queen Elizabeth used Thomas Baroncelli to keep her informed about fashion in Italy and to have clothes made for her. When he sent her some 'patterns of bodices' in 1565, the Earl of Leicester wrote back explaining that they were not what was wanted as she already had several of that type. He goes on to explain that the Queen really wanted the 'kind used in Spain and Italy, worked with gold and silver . . . I will send the pattern and measure'.[8]

The difficulty that the Shrewsbury tailor encountered in finding the right material in a small country town must have been shared by countless men and women throughout England and so it is easy to imagine the excitement when a member of a country family visited London and sent his purchases back home. When Philip Gawdy visited London on business in 1587, his sisters had briefed him to send the fullest possible account of what the ladies at court were wearing and instructed him to search out the best material to send back to them. On reading his letters one sympathises with his bewilderment as he tries to work out which fashion he should describe and then buy. A letter dated 11 April 1589 to his younger sister explains: 'I fynd nothing more certayne than their uncertaynty, which made me forbeare to send you anything further of myne owne devise until I have further from you.' He writes to his sister Ann in December 1587 to let her know that he has bought some damask that he feels 'will prove wondrous well' for her new gown, and goes on to explain that Fox (presumably the tailor) 'cannot tell in what manner to patterne it, neither needs it, for I can assure you that bothe the queene and all the gentlewomen at the courte weare the very fashion of yor tuff taffeta gowne with an open wired sleeve and such a cutt, and it is now the newest fashion'. Philip was extremely careful to find the best quality material at the most reasonable price and he also kept a close eye on the accessories worn at Court so that his sisters should have the most fashionable available. In 1593 he writes that he has sent his sister the items that she requested, a fan with a handle 'not stale (in) any kinde of waye, a fuardingall of the best fashion, gold thread, heare call (caul), her pumpes'.[9]

The tailor had a dishonest reputation at this time, as it was felt that he promoted the eccentricities of fashion for his own profit and perhaps also kept a portion of the customer's material for his own use. His involvement in shady dealings is well illustrated in an exchange between John and a tailor in Eliot's French conversation manual, *The Parlement of Prattlers*, 1598. A customer orders a doublet, breeches and cloak and offers the tailor a crown to buy the relevant trimmings – but if that does not cover it he is to steal the rest. The tailor is affronted and replies that he is not a thief and to this the customer answers, 'you are a tailor by your trade and a theefe by your occupation',[10] and leaves the shop.

Tailoring was not a highly paid trade (the tailors of the Great Wardrobe received 6d a day – the same rate as a skilled artisan but twice as much as a labourer), and great difficulty was often experienced when the tailor tried to extract payment for his work from the gallants, as they were notoriously slow to settle their debts. It was an accepted part of fashionable behaviour to delay paying the tailor for as long as possible, an attitude which is made plain in an exchange between two gallants in Dekker's play *The Honest Whore*, 1604. Matheo explains that he has played 'the gentleman's part' with his tailor by owing him money and when his friend asks why he should want to do that, Matheo replies:

> To keepe the fashion: it's your onely fashion now of your best ranke of gallants, to make their tailors waite for their money neither were it wisedome indeed to pay them upon the first edition of a new suite; for commonly the suite is owing for, when the lynings are worne out, and there's no reason then that the tailor should be paid before the mercer. (Part 2:IV.i.8)

Mercers specialized in costly imported materials and the variety that they offered was infinite. There were the glossy fabrics like satin, tabine, sarcenet, chamlet and taffeta. The latter could also be tufted, that is, woven with raised stripes or spots which, when cut, would leave a pile. As the pile was different from the ground, exquisite combinations of colour were possible. This treatment could also be applied to velvet, and if the pile was of different depths but of the same colour, beautiful variations of tone were created according to the way the light fell on it. Cloth of gold, cloth of silver, tinsel and tissue were the most luxurious fabrics, as they were woven with gold or silver thread so that they shone and sparkled. The temptations that the mercers offered fashionable young gentlemen were so powerful that by the end of the sixteenth century the word mercer became synonymous with their debts. 'Divers young gentlemen shall creep further into the mercers book in a moneth than they can get out in a yeere'.[11]

In *The French Garden*, 1605, Lady Beau-Sejour argues with a mercer over the price of 'cloth of gold', for which he wants £4 a yard and she offers only £3. The mercer finally agrees on that price as she is a good customer and wants ten yards. The average price was between £1 and £3 a yard depending on quality; this price compares with ten to twenty shillings a yard for tabine, about £2 a yard for tissue, four to five shillings a yard for sarcenet, three to fourteen shillings for satin, ten to fifteen shillings for taffeta and twenty to thirty-four shillings for velvet. Prices were dependent on the quality of the fabric and whether it was embellished with embroidery or spangles.

The shops of the most exclusive mercers were situated in Cheapside and from their customer's account-books we know that the most fashionable were owned by Sir William Stone (the Kytsons used his shop for their daughter's wedding) and Sir Baptist Hicks. Sir Baptist Hicks, whose shop was at the sign of 'The Whyte Bear' at the junction of Sopers Lane and Cheapside, was a spectacularly successful mercer who made a fortune out of his trade. The high standard of goods sold in his shop was ensured by factors at Leghorn and Florence who procured the finest Italian fabrics without going through an intermediary. Hicks' customer list reads like an Elizabethan *Who's Who*, for it includes Queen Elizabeth, Thomas Hatton (nephew of Sir Christopher Hatton), Robert Cecil and his son Thomas, Charles Howard the Lord Admiral, Antony Throckmorton (Raleigh's brother-in-law) and Sir Francis Bacon.

A draper sold high-quality woollen goods: 'fine cloth, of serge, of bays, of kersye',[12] or, if he was a linen draper, stocked high-quality cotton goods. William Ferrers was a

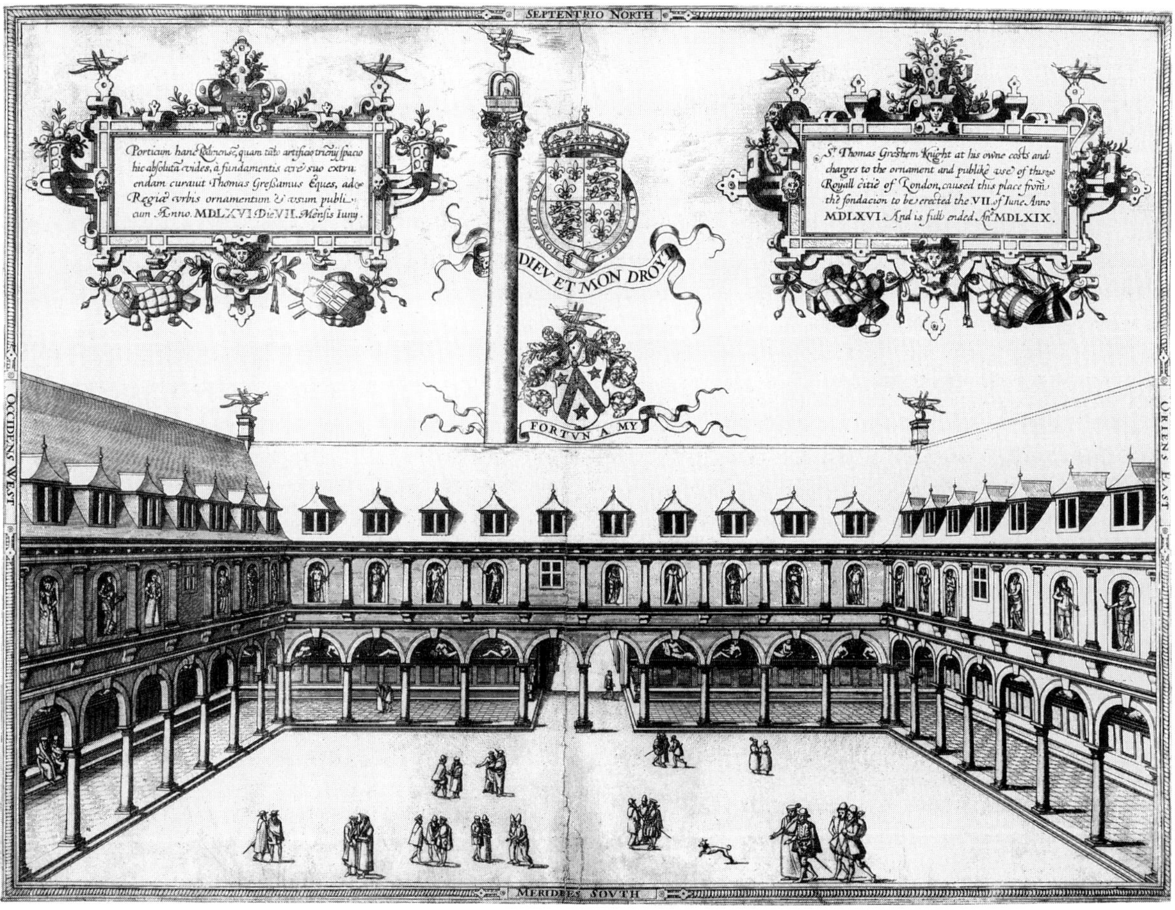

50. *Engraving by Francis Hogenberg of The Royal Exchange, 1569.* (By courtesy of the Trustees of the British Museum)

linen draper who dealt in imported fine linens and he was the main supplier to the Great Wardrobe and the Queen herself.

Fashion accessories, sold by haberdashers, were divided into two types of merchandise: hats and small wares. In the sixteenth century the purveyor of small wares became known as a milliner, a title derived from his merchandise which was originally mainly imported from Milan. This merchandise included bracelets, brooches, jewels, fans, garters, wigs, gloves and a certain number of ready-made garments, usually linen ruffs, cuffs, shirts and embroidered waistcoats. Thus the milliner's stock became more and more varied and could also be very expensive. By the end of James I's reign their shops were 'stored with rich and curious imbroydered Waistcoats of the full value of some tenne pound apiece, twentie and some forty pound'.[13] Also stocked were perfumes, scented gloves and powder, which gave the milliner a rather effeminate image.

> He was perfumed like a milliner
> And twixt his finger and his thumb he held
> A pouncet-box, which ever and anon
> He gave his nose, and took't away again'.[14]

The milliner's stalls and many other fashion stalls were located in the Pawn at the Royal Exchange (*50*). The Exchange became a byword in contemporary literature as a treasure-house of desirable goods and the meeting place for fashionable society:

> . . . there's her embossings,
> Embroderings, spanglings, and I know not what,
> As if she lay with all the gaudy-shops
> In Gresham's Burse about her'.[15]

It was the place to visit to buy presents as well as personal adornments. When the pious Lady Hoby visited London, on 30 December 1600, she noted in her diary that

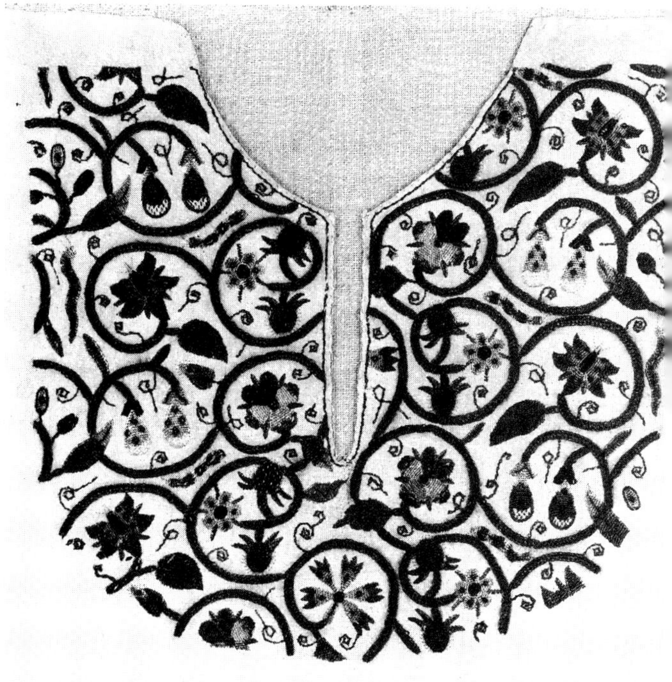

51. Child's partlet, coloured silks on linen. Late sixteenth century. (By courtesy of the Board of Trustees of the Victoria & Albert Museum, London)

she went to 'the Exchange to buy a new years gift'.[16] The choice of gifts to be found there was enormous, as this list from Breton's *The Fort of Fancy*, 1577, intimates:

> Such purses, gloves and points
> Of cost and fashion rare,
> Such cutworks, partlets, suits of lawn,
> Bongraces and such ware;
> Such gorgets, sleeves and ruffs,
> Linings for gowns and cauls,
> Coifs, crippins, cornets, billaments,
> Musk boxes and sweet balls;
> Pincases, pick-tooths, beard-brushes,
> Combs, needles, glasses, bells.[17]

A child's partlet in the Victoria & Albert Museum (*51*) is in a particularly good state of preservation and gives a clear idea of what a ready-made partlet must have

52. Elizabeth Vernon, The Countess of Southampton. Unknown artist, 1595–1600. (By permission of The Duke of Buccleuch and Queensberry)

looked like. The plain border round the embroidery would not have been seen, as it would be pinned to the undergarment. An ivory comb endearingly labelled *Menez moi doucement* is held by the Countess of Southampton in a portrait by an unknown artist (*52*) which affords a rare glimpse of domesticity. Her pincushion, a vital article since pins united most garments, rests next to her jewel box and its elaborate contents. Displayed on the curtain is a circular ruff with gauze ruching and beneath it a decoration for a stomacher, a circling pattern of enamelled white flowers interspersed with black and red jewels set in gold. As she is in the privacy of her dressing-room, the Countess wears a strikingly embroidered jacket (also called a waistcoat) with bright pink ribbon ties. As mentioned before, these garments could be bought ready-made in the Exchange and elsewhere. A number of these garments have survived and one is in the Burrell Collection in Glasgow (see colour pl. 8). The brilliantly coloured design of flowers, butterflies and birds has been worked with coloured silks and plaited gold braid on a cream linen ground.

An example of the sort of gloves that would have been for sale in the Exchange can be found in the Ashmolean Museum (*53*), where a pair of embroidered kid gloves, presented to the Queen when she visited Oxford University, have been preserved. They are of the highest quality and give an

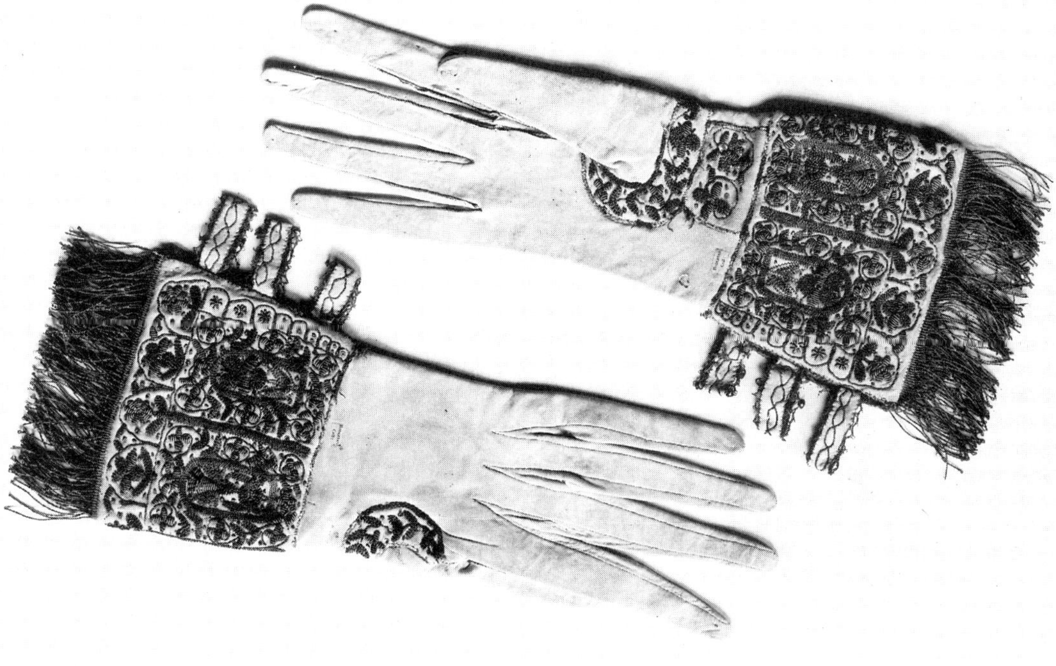

53. Embroidered kid gloves. Late sixteenth century. (The Ashmolean Museum, Oxford)

indication of the length of the Queen's fingers.

The Royal Exchange was so famous an institution that Thomas Heywood wrote a play about it, *The Faire Maide of the Exchange*, 1607.[18] This gives a very detailed picture of the way the different stalls operated and the services they offered to the fashionable customer, ranging from the starchers who stiffened linen garments, through suppliers of hat feathers, to 'attyre makers'. The latter designed and arranged women's hairstyles, an occupation which, judging from references in contemporary drama, was thankless and exasperating. The main character, the Faire Maide, is an apprentice to a seamstress in the Exchange. Seamstresses specialized in the making and sale of linen garments, unlike the milliner who offered a wider range of goods. The stall in the play offers the choice

> Of lawnes, or cambricks, ruffes well wrought, shirts,
> Fine falling bands, of the Italian cut-worke,
> Ruffes for your hands, wast-coates wrought with silke,
> Nightcaps of gold, or such like wearing linen.
> (III.i.69–72)

Falling bands could be bought either as a separate item or already attached to the shirt. An example of the latter can be found in the accounts of the Earl of Rutland, who in 1596 bought a shirt 'with a cutworke bande ready made' for 50 shillings.[19] Cutwork was of Italian origin and was made by cutting shapes from the background fabric and then filling the spaces with geometric designs of needle lace. Cutwork could also be edged with purl (a needle-made lace of silk, silver or gold). Fastidious Brisk, a character in Jonson's *Every Man out of his Humour*, boasts that he paid £3 in the Exchange for an Italian cutwork collar

54. Unknown man. Nicholas Hilliard, 1588. (By courtesy of the Board of Trustees of the Victoria & Albert Museum, London)

edged with purl.[20] The dramatic effect of a cutwork collar against the dark background of a doublet can be gauged in Hilliard's miniature of an unknown man (*54*). An even more elaborate and entirely needle-made lace was the Italian *punto in aria*, and an example of its use as an edging to a ruff can be seen in a portrait of the Countess of Argyll (*55*).

Embroidered and spangled nightcaps were worn indoors with a nightgown when the wearer wanted to relax and feel comfortable. They were usually embroidered at home, but if a particularly impressive cap was required they could be bought ready-

55. The Countess of Argyll. Unknown artist, 1599. (National Galleries of Scotland)

ÆTATIS

made. According to Frances, Countess of Hereford, who wrote to her steward in London in 1603, the best embroiderer of nightcaps was 'Mrs Price in the Strand'. The Countess instructed him to buy a 'very fair one and not grossly wrought', it was to be 'black silke and golde and silver' and the price did not matter, although she did point out that when she last bought one it cost about £3.[21] Many nightcaps have survived, and one with an unusual design of snakes and obelisks is in the Chertsey Museum (*56*). The spangles that decorate it are clearly visible. Interestingly, the same design is featured on the skirt of Queen Elizabeth in the portrait at Cowdray (*21*).

The most exclusive jewellers and goldsmiths were concentrated in Goldsmiths Row, an imposing edifice built in 1491 and described by Stow in his *Survey of London* as 'the most beautiful frame of fayre houses and shoppes, that bee within the walles of London'.[22] Goldsmiths and jewellers fulfilled two functions in Elizabethan society, the first being to design and make the objects that were offered for sale, and the second being to act as a banker. Using the client's own jewels as security, money would be loaned at an annual interest rate which varied between 10 and 12 per cent. If the client wanted to travel abroad, the goldsmith could provide letters of credit and foreign currency. Peter Vandelore (also called Valore) was a famous jeweller/banker in late sixteenth- and early seventeenth-century London. He was patronized by Queen Elizabeth, King James, the Earl of Hertford, Sir Walter Raleigh and the Earl of Rutland. The latter used him as a supplier of foreign currency when he visited France and Italy in the 1590s and purchased from him in 1586 a 'brooch of her Majestie's picture in an aggatt sett with 53 diamonds',

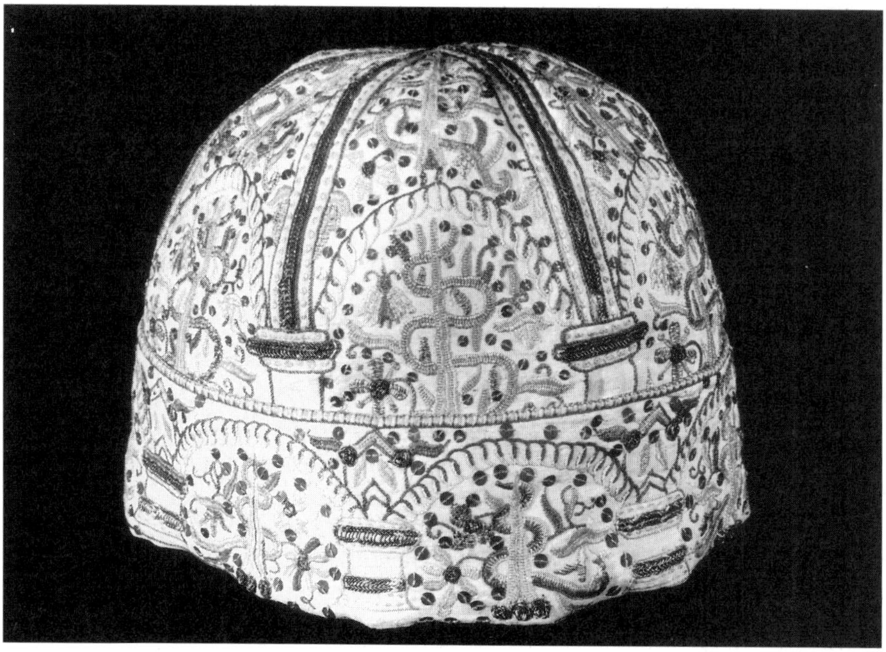

56. Embroidered nightcap. Coloured silks and metal thread on linen. Late sixteenth century. (Chertsey Museum)

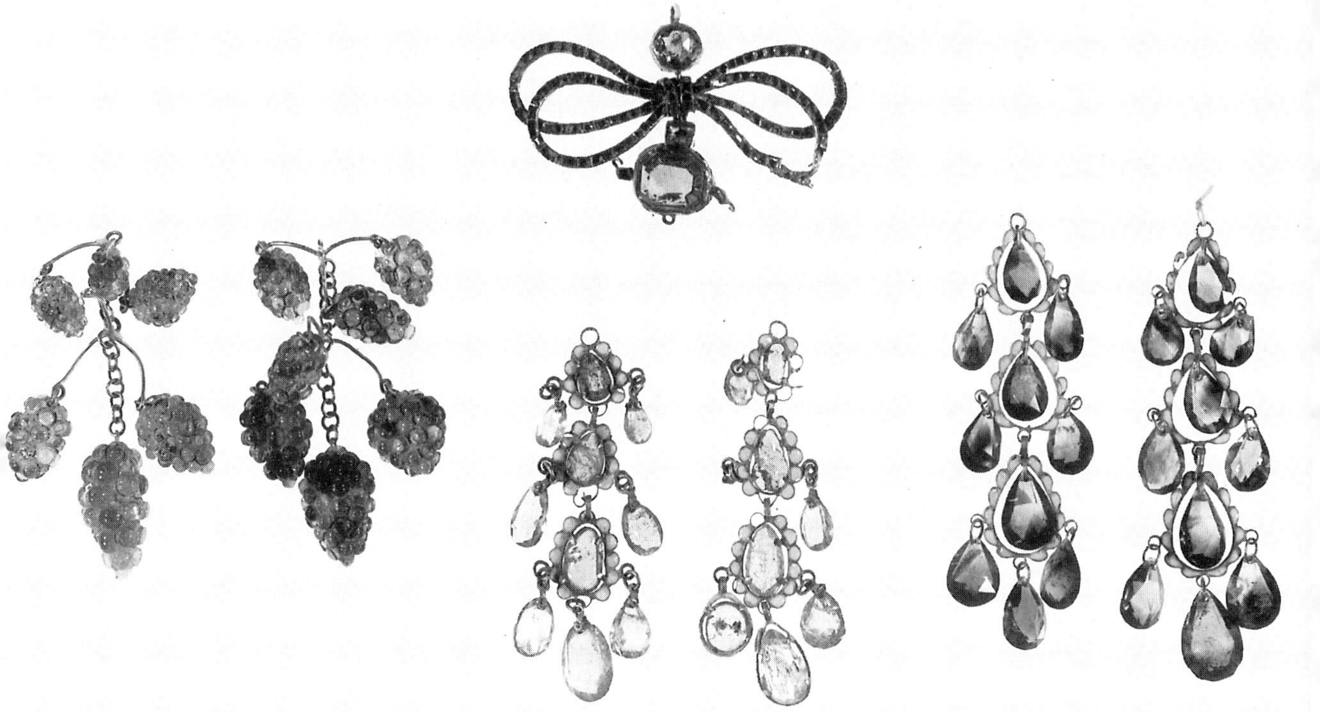

57. The Cheapside Hoard. Gold pendant in form of bow, pendants of amethysts carved as grapes, emerald and amethyst drop pendants. Late sixteenth century. (The Museum of London)

at a cost of £80.[23] William Herrick (father of the poet Robert) was another extremely successful goldsmith. He was held in high regard by the Queen, made Principal Jeweller to King James in 1603 and knighted in 1605. His shop was visited by the parents of Mary Kytson when they were buying her wedding trousseau in 1583. They paid to Mr Herycke, goldsmith, in Cheapside for a 'cheyne of gold sett with perle, for my Lady Darcy £47'. They also visited Vandelore, from whom they bought a 'greate perle' at a cost of £30.[24] Jewellery, if in the form of a pendant or a brooch, would not be confined to the bodice or doublet; it could be pinned to a ruff, the hair or a hatband. A splendid example of the first two uses can be seen in the portrait of the Countess of Argyll (*55*), who wears a massive pendant on her ruff and another in her hair.

Fortunately, part of the stock of one of the Cheapside jewellers has survived, and is now on display in the Museum of London. It is a fascinating collection that affords a unique glimpse into the world of one Elizabethan shopkeeper. The collection was discovered by a workman in 1912 and comprises chains, rings, fanholders, hairpins, buttons, pendants, a pomander and a number of unset gems (*57, 58, 59*). The stock is not of the quality of that owned by Herrick

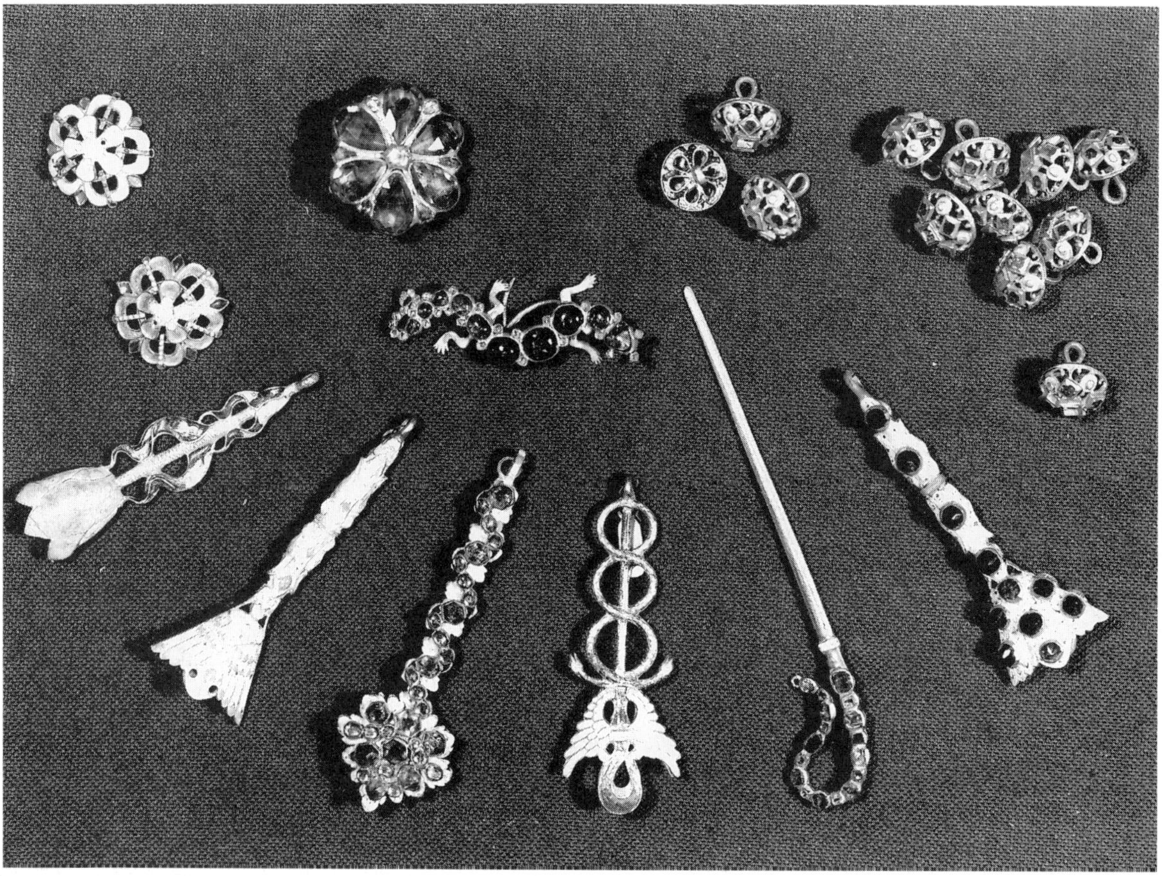

58. The Cheapside Hoard. Fan holder, hairpin (bodkin), fan holder in form of caduceus, three enamelled fan holders, hat ornament in form of salamander, circular hat ornaments, gold enamelled buttons. Late sixteenth century. (The Museum of London)

and Vandelore and it is likely that it would have been aimed at middle-class rather than aristocratic customers.

The area of St Martins Le Grand had privileges of sanctuary for 'strangers born' and so had a large immigrant population, mainly of Dutch, French and German, who pursued their trades of pursemaking, tailoring, millinery, lacemaking and buttonmaking. It was the place to visit if you wanted to buy lace, cheap jewellery and shoes. Sir Thomas Overbury wrote cynically about an 'affected traveller' who bought his jewellery in St Martins and after he 'pronounced them worth thousands, empawneth them for a few shillings'.[25]

Supplying a fur or lining a garment with fur was a specialist service (*60*) available in Budge Row where the skinners worked, the road adopting its name from the fur known as budge (lambskin with the wool dressed outwards). The most successful skinner was Adam Bland, and later his son Peter, both of whom were patronized by the Queen for many years. An account of the work that Adam Bland did for Henry Sidney, the father of Sir Philip, in 1570–71 has survived, and is an interesting indication of the type of work that was undertaken. In 1570 Bland charged 3s. 4d to line a 'long gown of wrought velvet' with sable fur that cost £3. The following year a satin gown was lined with lynx at a total cost of £10, a short gown lined with Spanish fox cost £5 10s. and a cloth gown was furred with black cony and white lamb for 4 shillings. The total bill over a two-year period came to £66 6s. 11d.[26]

Since clothes were a visible display of wealth, a man was usually judged by the value of the suit he wore. If a man could not afford to have a new suit made he could buy second-hand clothes in Birchin Lane, but to do so was a mark of social inferiority: 'his discourse makes not his behaviour but he buyes it at court, as country men buy their clothes in Birchin Lane'.[27] The range of garments on sale was enormous, for it was

59. The Cheapside Hoard. Enamelled gold chains set with amethysts and emeralds. Late sixteenth century. (The Museum of London)

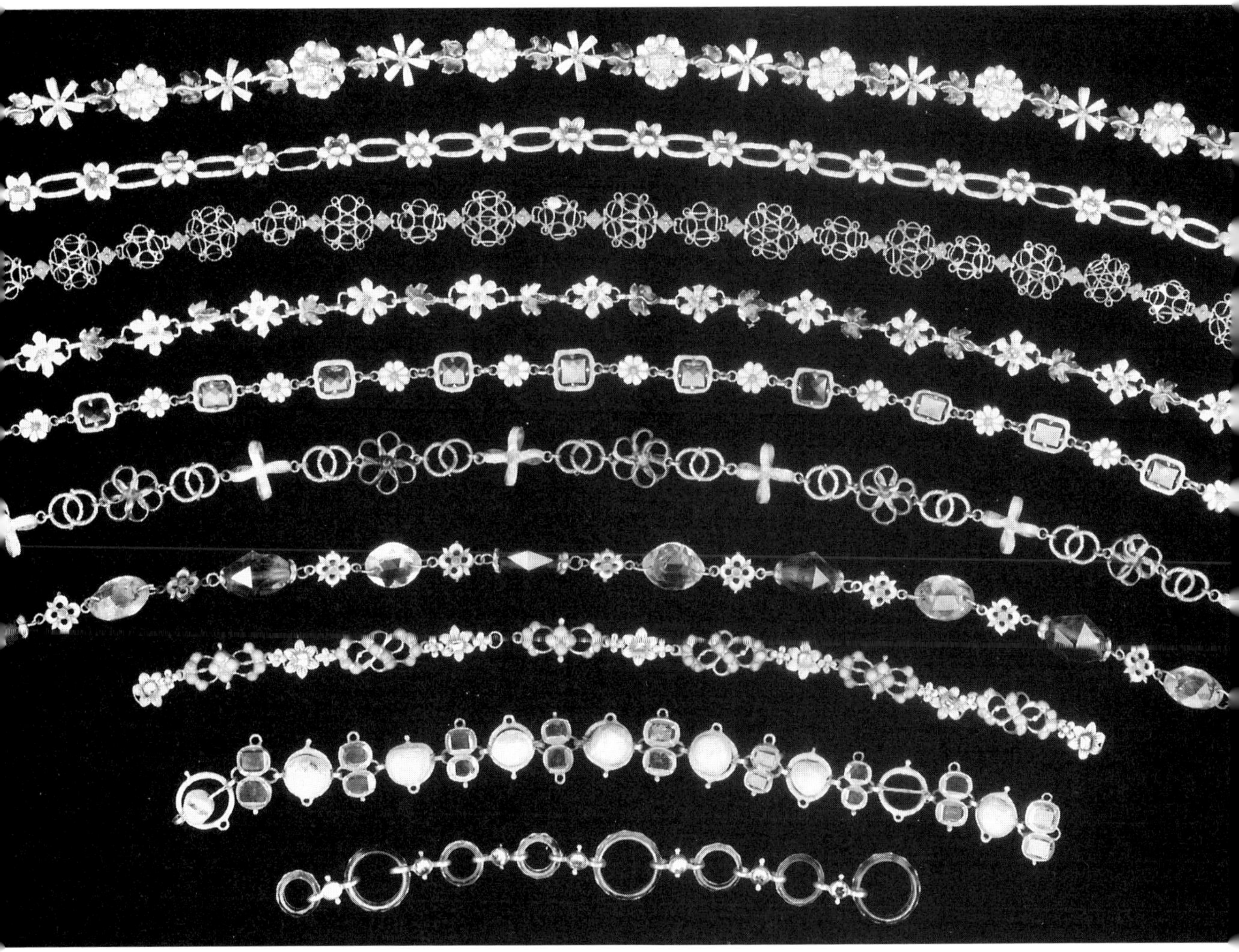

60. The Furrier, from Eygentliche Beschreibung aller Standeauff, *Jost Amman, Frankfurt, 1568.* (By courtesy of the Board of Trustees of the Victoria & Albert Museum, London)

possible to buy clothes which had belonged to men of all social classes and professions. Middleton's description of a captain's suit bought in Birchin Lane is typical of the ostentatious taste of the military, 'a valiant buff doublet, stuffed with points like a leg of mutton with parsley and a pair of velvet slops scored thick with lace, which ran round about the hose like ringworms, able to make a man scratch where it itched not'.[28] Although fashionable second-hand dress was on sale in Birchin Lane, the poor frequented Houndsditch and Old Jewry where the 'fripperers' sold older, more tattered clothes.

The violent attack of the Plague in 1603 caused a severe setback to trade in Birchin Lane and tailoring in general. In the broadsheet of that year, *Meeting of gallants at an ordinarie*, the gallants wear their 'old sutes', for they dare not have anything new made in case the material is infected. Clothes bought in Birchin Lane were particularly suspect, for 'there is as much perill betweene the wings and the skirts of one of their doublets' as there is in 'all the most infected places of England'.[29]

Experience and knowledge of fashion in country areas was shaped by visits to annual fairs and by inspection of the pedlar's wares. Shakespeare, in his portrait of Autolycus in *The Winter's Tale*, gives a composite picture of the wide range of goods that these itinerant salesmen offered. The stage direction in IV.iii.220 brings on Autolycus, singing:

> Lawn as white as driven snow
> Cyprus, black as e'er was crow;
> Gloves, as sweet as damask roses;
> Masks for faces, and for noses;
> Bugle-bracelet, necklace-amber,
> Perfume for a lady's chamber;
> Golden quoifs, and stomachers,
> For my lads to give their dears;
> Pins and poking-sticks of steel . . .

Autolycus's description of his gloves as 'sweet as roses' means that they were perfumed. Spanish perfumed or 'washed' gloves were considered to be the finest available, and in the play *Sir Giles Goosecap* one of the characters boasts that he knows a man who will 'perfume your gloves himselfe; most delicately, and give them the right Spanish titillation' (II.i.979). The housewife could perform the operation for herself, in which case the most popular perfumes to use were benjamin, jasmine and orange water, but once a pair of gloves had been treated it was virtually impossible to remove the scent. Autolycus's song tells us that he also sold perfume, cheaper items of jewellery, poking sticks to shape ruffs, and some ready-made accessories such as coifs, stomachers and smocks with embroidery on the sleeve-hand. Pedlars carried a variety of dress trimmings, ribbons 'of all the colours i' the rainbow', braids and a selection of laces. His pack would almost certainly have included bride lace, a bobbin-made lace which was tied on the wedding cup or on nosegays at weddings.

Those who lived near a fairly large country town were fortunate, as generally the range of trimmings, materials and accessories was quite wide. This is demonstrated by the inventory of goods stocked by James Backhouse, who lived in Kirby Lonsdale in 1578. He could offer his customers a choice of woollen fabrics, red, turkey and brown-blue frizado, sky, russet, green, gilliflower, 'sad new colour' (any dark shade) and white kersey, black and green motley and blue-black bays (baize). Cloths of silk-and-linen and wool-and-linen included mockado, boratto, carells, rash, fustian and bustian. The only silks he stocked were cyprus and sarcenet, but if linen were required he could provide lawn, cambric and holland. He carried a large range of embroidery silks and lace and four types of points. Hats, hatbands, combs, thimbles, garters, gloves, nightcaps and buttons were available alongside household goods, spices and dried fruit.[30]

Only the aristocratic few like the imaginary Lady Ri-Mellaine in *The French Garden* would visit a mercer's shop and be able to buy expensive new material or spend £180 on one gown, as Mary Ratcliffe did in 1597 when she made her first appearance at court.[31] The majority of Englishwomen made their own clothes and would rarely buy new ones. Changes in fashion would be acknowledged by an alteration in the shape of an existing garment or the addition of a new trimming or accessory.

Chapter Four

"Printing my thoughts in lawn": the language of dress

Expression of an abstract idea through a visual image was an essential part of Elizabethan life, for the love of allegory was all-pervasive and an accepted part of everyday life. Allegorical figures would appear in tournaments, street pageants, masques and poems, and the abstract idea that their appearance symbolized would be immediately identified and enjoyed by the spectator or reader. The close relationship that was felt to exist between image and meaning was an inevitable result of a belief that art and literature were sister arts and as such were interchangeable and could be judged by identical standards. It was this perception of closeness that led the Elizabethans to regard poetry as a 'speaking picture with this end to teach and delight',[1] a didactic purpose which was also applied to the decorative arts and even to clothes. The attitude is made clear in this description of embroidery:

> Sir, she is a Puritan at her needle too . . .
> My smock sleeves have such holy embroideries,
> And are so learned, that I fear in time
> All my apparell will be quoted by
> Some pure instructor . . .[2]

The obvious implication is that the smock has been embroidered with motifs that have a moral or religious significance.

Allegory appears in the decorative arts in two ways: by use of either an emblem or a device. Emblem books originated in Italy in the 1530s, and although they were enjoyed by English intellectuals they did not have a wide circulation in England until the publication of the first emblem book in English, Geoffrey Whitney's *A choice of emblems*, 1586. From that point on a common visual vocabulary was available to everyone; as Rosemary Freeman points out in her book *English Emblem Books*, 'the great merit of the Elizabethan emblem books is that they could be set in such a variety of contexts with so little alteration and that while a courtly Euphues was poring over one emblem book to find witty ideas with which to enliven his conversation, his wife was embroidering his coat from another'.[3]

The emblem comprised an engraving of a picture, a set of verses and a motto which encapsulated the meaning of both picture and verse. The motto usually expressed a general moral truth, and many have remained in our language as proverbs. The example from Whitney (*61*) has the motto

The Adder lurketh privilie in the Grass, with an accompanying verse that points out the danger of falling for flattery and 'sugared wordes'. The phrase 'a snake in the grass' is a direct derivation and it is interesting that the emblem can also be seen in the top left-hand corner of 'The Shepherd Buss' *63*. The concise linear nature of the emblem and its attractive pictorial qualities meant that it had a particular appeal for the embroiderer, as it was easy to transfer to a piece of material. To achieve this the printed image would be placed on top of the material, the outline would be pricked through with a pin, powdered charcoal or cuttlefish bone would be dusted through the holes, and when the picture was removed a clear outline would remain behind. An excellent example of the way emblems were incorporated into embroidery can be found in the Falkland jacket in the Victoria & Albert Museum (*62*). It is a blackwork jacket, that is, the ground of white linen has been worked with black silk thread. As is common with much surviving blackwork, its condition is poor. The encircling floral pattern encloses within its leaves flowers, fruits, animals, insects and a number of emblems taken from Whitney's books. The emblems include the child Hercules holding a snake and riding a crocodile, Bacchus

61. An emblem from Geoffrey Whitney's A Choice of Emblems, *London, 1586*

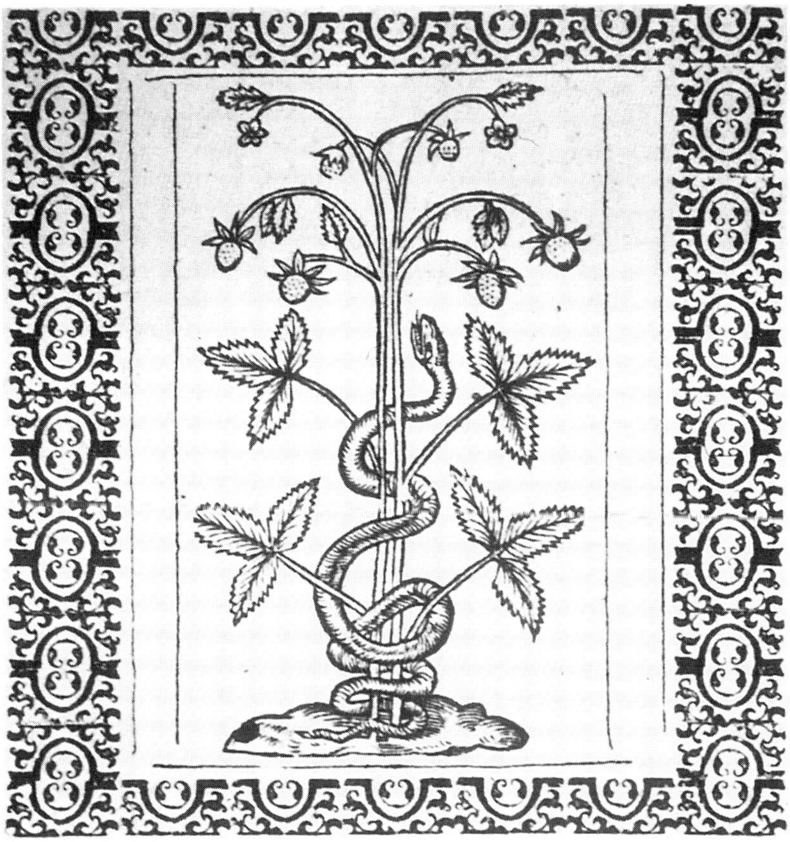

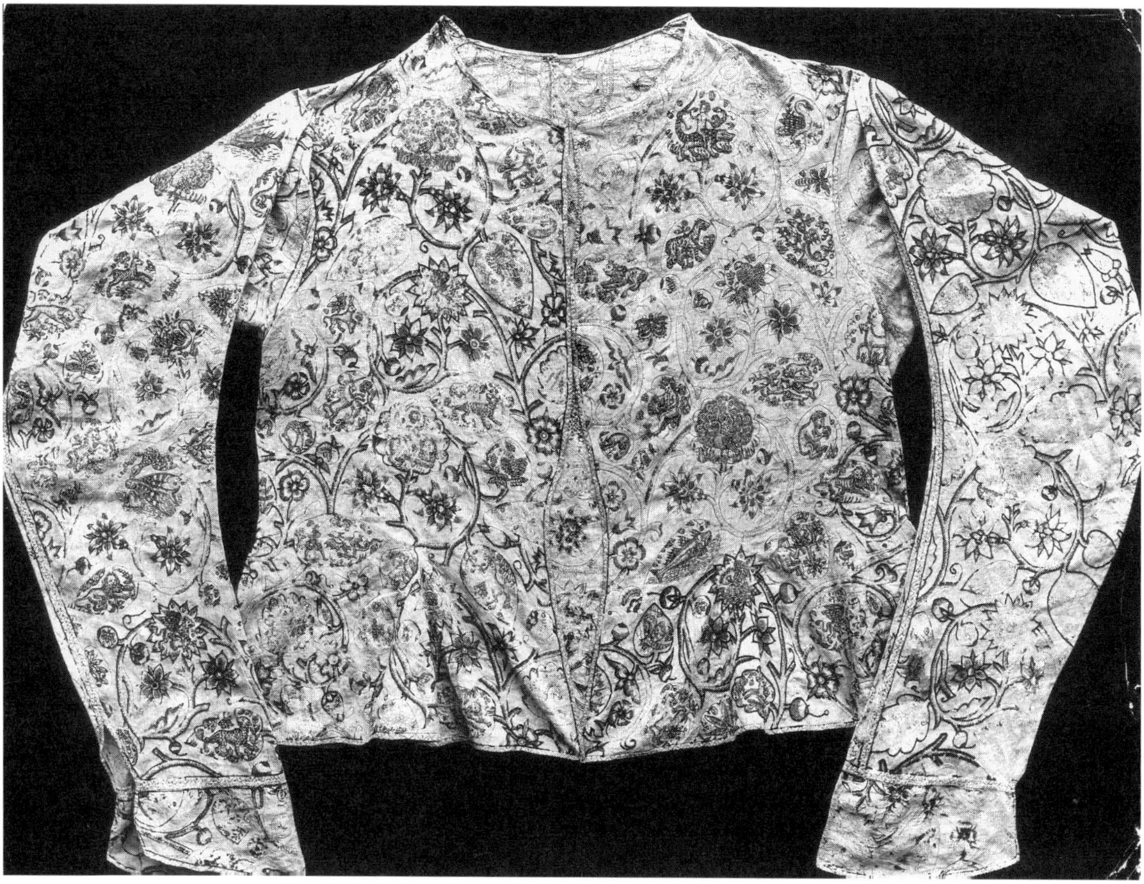

62. The 'Falkland Jacket'. Black silk on white linen. Late sixteenth century. (By courtesy of the Board of Trustees of the Victoria & Albert Museum, London)

with a drum, and Aceton. Other instances of Whitney's emblems can be found worked into mediums as diffuse as plaster, silver, tapestry, wood and even painted on glass (see the Vyvyan Salt, 1592–3, in the Victoria & Albert Museum).

In the play *The Faire Maide of the Exchange* we learn much about the production of embroidery and how it was used to convey a message. One of the characters in the play, Moll Berry, goes to the Royal Exchange to consult with a 'drawer' because she cannot decide on a pattern for a handkerchief destined for her lover. The 'drawer' would produce patterns on garments or any piece of material so that the customer could then embroider them. Moll's choice of imagery is typical of the Elizabethan love of allegory and 'dark conceit':

> In one corner of the same, place wanton Love,
> Drawing his bow shooting an amorous dart,
> Opposite him an arrow in a heart,
> In a third corner, picture forth disdaine,
> A cruel fate unto a loving vaine:
> In the fourth draw a springing Laurel-tree,
> Circled about with a ring of poesie: and thus it is:
> Love wounds the heart, and conquers fell disdaine.
> (V.i.557–65)

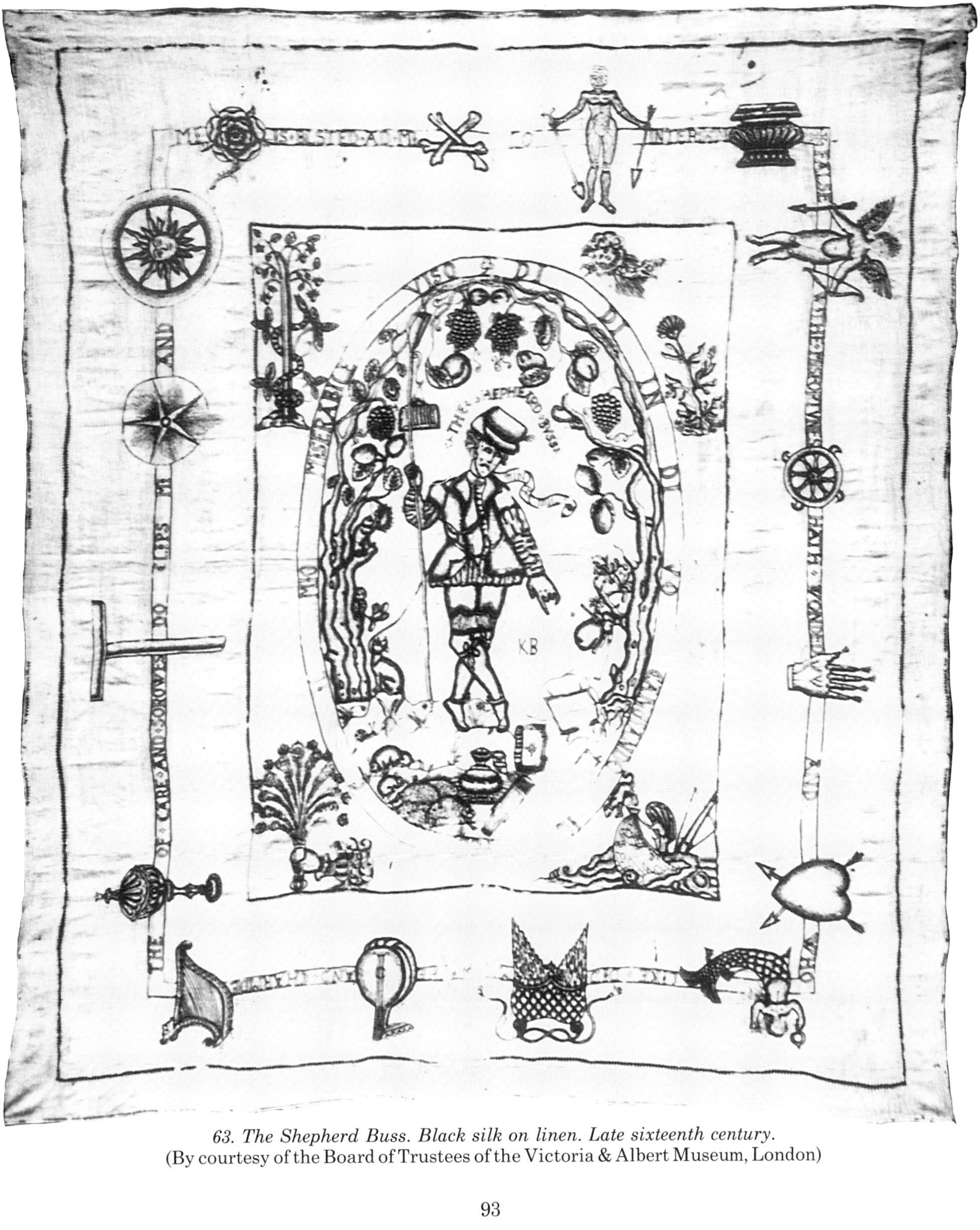

63. The Shepherd Buss. Black silk on linen. Late sixteenth century.
(By courtesy of the Board of Trustees of the Victoria & Albert Museum, London)

There is a close parallel between this description of a design and the motifs embroidered on a coverlet in the Victoria & Albert Museum, known as 'The Shepherd Buss' (*63*). The central oval depicts a lovelorn shepherd standing under an arbour made of vines; this scene is enclosed within a rectangle which has an emblem situated in each of the four corners. The inscription round the outer border, in the form of rebus devices (a way of composing a sentence by substituting a picture for the noun), has a melancholic message:

> False cupid with misfortunes wheel hath wounded hand and heart
> Who sirenlike did lure me withe lute and charmide harp.
> The cup of care and sorrowes cross do clips mi star and sun
> Mi rose is bl(a)sted a (n)d mi bones lo death inters in urn.

The portrait of Edward, Lord Russell (*64*), 1573, is an interesting example of the way that symbols could be incorporated into a painting to convey a personal message, the meaning of which is now lost. Edward, dressed in a fashionable outfit of matching cloak and hose and slashed doublet, incongruously holds in his hand a bunch of writhing snakes from whose mouths flutters a message. In the top left-hand corner of the portrait there is another enigmatic image, that of a solitary figure standing in the middle of a maze-like pattern within a garden.

The extraordinarily elaborate embroidery patterns that were popular made the services of a professional pattern drawer essential, but if a drawer was not available a design could be pricked for copying. Examples of this practice can be seen in Jacques Lemoine's book *La Clef des Champs*, 1586. It contains 98 woodcuts of

64. Lord Edward Russell. Unknown artist, 1573. (By kind permission of the Marquess of Tavistock and the Trustees of the Bedford Estates)

animals, birds, flowers, plants and fruit, and many of the plates in the British Library copy of the book have been pricked through. The book was dedicated to Lady Mary Sidney (*20*) and Lemoine hoped it would serve not only those interested in embroidery but also goldsmiths and tapestry makers, all of whom depended on the work of painters. Other sources of subject and pattern were herbal and flower paintings, natural history books, engravings and woodcuts of Biblical and mythological subjects. There were earlier pattern books but until the beginning of the seventeenth century these were for lace work. The earliest pattern book for the embroiderer was Thomas Trevelyon's two large manuscript volumes, dated 1615, which offered a wide range of embroidery patterns.[4]

The most spectacular embroidered garments were those given to Queen Elizabeth on New Year's Day, when it was the tradition for all at court to give the Queen a gift commensurate with their social position. Motifs drawn from the four elements, including clouds, rainbows, flames and suns, were very popular and occur in different combinations in the Great Wardrobe inventories and gift lists. In the 1600 inventory is listed a forepart of cloth of silver, which must have been particularly impressive since it was 'embrodred all over with Rainebowes cloudes flames of fire and sonnes of silke of sondrie colours'.[5] Also listed is a cloak of tawny satin which was embroidered on the shoulders 'like a cloude with sonnebeames and rainbowes the rest embrodred with hawthorne trees essefirmes cyphers hopes and other devyses'.[6] An em-

Æ^T · SVÆ · 22
Edward Lord Russell 1st
Son of the Francis Earle
of Bedford
A · VIAM · INVENIENT

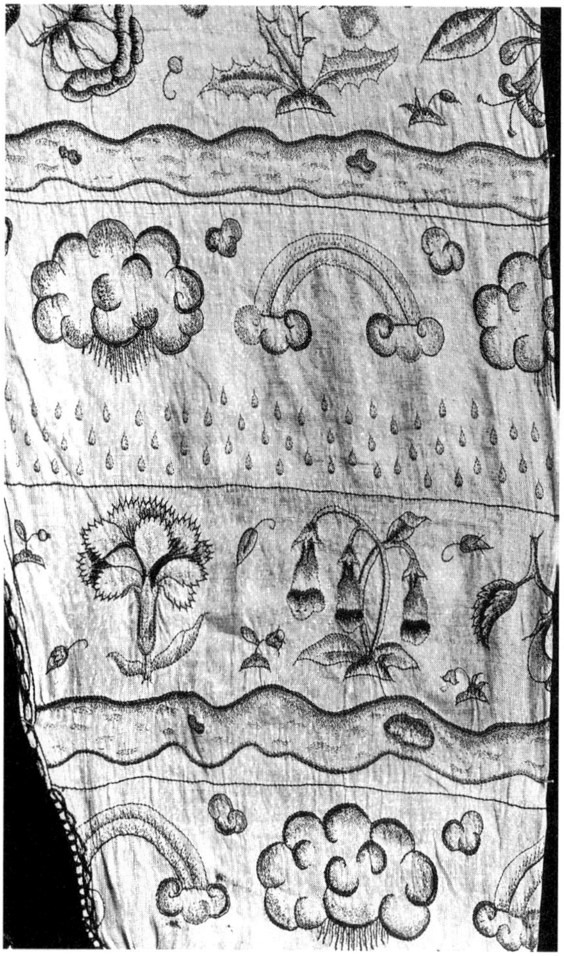

65. Embroidered smock. Coloured silks on linen. Late sixteenth century. (Whitworth Art Gallery, Manchester)

broidered smock in the Whitworth Art Gallery in Manchester and a nightcap in the Cooper-Hewitt Museum, New York, (*65, 66*) give an idea of the possible appearance of the patterns on Elizabeth's forepart and cloak. The smock is embroidered in coloured silks with clouds and rainbows above a border of raindrops; this design alternates with a band of flowers. The cap is embroidered with brightly coloured rainbows, storm clouds, snails, and caterpillars. A likely origin for the motif of a dense cloud disgorging drops of rain can be found in Claude Paradin's *Devises Heroiques* (*67*). First published in France in 1557 and translated into English in 1591, it was a popular sourcebook for the Elizabethan embroiderer, and the emblems in 'The Shepherd Buss' are taken from the 1591 edition. A rainbow and raindrops also appear in Paradin as the device of Catherine de Medici, and are borrowed by Queen Elizabeth in the famous Rainbow portrait at Hatfield House (*92*). Henry Peacham copies it in his book *Minerva Britanna*, 1612 (*68*).

Among the more unusual and ambitious embroidered designs are 'dead trees flowers and a lyon in the myddest',[7] 'pomegranates, pyneapple trees, frutidge and the Nyne Muses',[8] 'peramyds, pillars and Muses in cloudes', with a border of 'clouds and pavallons',[9] a forepart of white satin embroidered with 'borders of the Sonne Mone and other signes and plannetts . . . with a border of Beastes beneath',[10] and finally a forepart embroidered 'like seas with dyvers devyses of rockes, shippes and fishes'.[11] An embroidered glove gauntlet in the Spence collection, now in the Museum of Costume, Bath, gives us some idea of the dramatic quality of this type of embroidery, for it shows a man in a garden of vines and a rocky island in a stream full of fish.

The life-like quality of contemporary embroidery is the subject of a rather wry comment in the anonymous play *Sir Giles Goosecap*, 1606, in which one character explains to two ladies that his embroiderer is so skilful that he

66. Embroidered nightcap. Coloured silks and metal thread on linen, 1590–1610. (Courtesy of the Cooper-Hewitt Museum, Smithsonian Institution Art Resource, New York)

67. Claude Paradin, Devises Heroiques, *Paris, 1557*

> will work you any flower to the life, as like it as if it grew in the very place, and being a delicate perfumer, he will give it you his perfect and natural savour . . . He will make you flies and worms of all sorts, most liuely, and is now working a whole bed embrodred with nothing but glow-wormes; whose lightes a has so perfectly done, that you may goe to bed in the chamber, doe anything in the chamber. (II.i.992–1002)

Embroidered flies, snails, snakes, worms and grasshoppers frequently appear on garments presented to the Queen. In 1580 Roger North, second Baron North of Kirtling, paid an embroiderer 50 shillings to enliven a pair of gloves for the Queen with 'froggs and flies'.[12] We know that the Queen had a white satin forepart in her Wardrobe that was embroidered with the somewhat bizarre design of spiders, flies and roundels with cobwebs.[13] In 1595 she wore a jewelled spider to create an even stranger *trompe l'oeil* effect, 'Her Majesty was this time dressed in a red robe interwoven with gold . . . over her breast . . . she wore a long filigree lace shawl, on which sat a hideous large black spider that looked as if it were natural and alive. Many might have been deceived by it.'[14]

Symbolism in dress is apparent in the choice of colour, embroidery pattern and flowers that were worn. Each flower and colour had a particular meaning, so its inclusion could be a statement of the wearer's mood. In nearly every portrait of the Queen there are flowers, whether fresh ones (*70*) or embroidered, and their appearance is usually for symbolic reasons. Being a Tudor, Elizabeth's association with the rose was obvious, for the double Tudor rose was a symbol of the union of the white rose of the House of York with the red rose of Lancaster. The lily and the eglantine were chosen because they were the flowers of purity and chastity. This connection was made plain when the Queen visited Bisham, home of Lady Russell, in 1591. During the course of the entertainment her daughters, Elizabeth and Anne Russell, dressed as shepherdesses, were found embroidering their samplers. When Pan asks them what they are embroidering, they reply, 'the honour of virgins who become goddesses for

68. Henry Peacham, Minerva Britanna, *London, 1612.* (By courtesy of the Trustees of the British Museum)

69. Frances Clinton, Lady Chandos. Hieronimo Custodis, 1589.
(By kind permission of the Marquess of Tavistock and the Trustees of the Bedford Estates)

their chastity', and the flowers that symbolize that are 'roses, eglantine, heartsease wrought with the Queens stitch'.[15] The same flowers were mentioned when the Queen was entertained in 1590 by Lord Burghley at Theobalds where she was taken into the garden and the gardener explained that he had planted 'all the Virtues, all the Graces, and all the Muses winding and wreathing about your Majesty . . . the Virtues were done in roses . . . the Graces of pansies party coloured . . . the Muses of several flowers . . . then I was commanded to place an arbour all of eglantine, in which my master's conceit outstripped my cunning'.[16]

The eglantine was a single, five-petalled rose which had been used in medieval art to celebrate the Virgin Mary, but which was used by the Elizabethans as an extension of the traditional rose imagery to suggest Elizabeth's singular virtue of chastity. It appears as a royal flower on jewellery, engravings, a glass painting at Loseley House, in court pageantry and in Hilliard's miniature of an unknown man leaning against a tree (*40*), in which it creates an exquisite pattern and serves as a complement to the Queen. The decorative potential of the eglantine, as well as its symbolism, must have appealed to the person who presented a white satin forepart to Elizabeth in 1600, embroidered with an 'eglantine tree spreading all over and flowers and leaves of Venice golde and silke'.[17]

Jewels in intricate settings designed as a 'dainty device' always pleased the Queen, and one that Baroness Howard gave her in 1584 sounds particularly fine: 'a Juell of golde beings a Dolfyne fully garnysshed with sparks of Rubyes with a personage uppon his backe having a Lute in his hande.'[18] A rather grandiose example of this type of jewellery can be found in the portrait of Frances Clinton, Lady Chandos, 1589 (*69*). On her bodice is pinned a large pendant depicting Perseus and Andromeda and on the wing of her left sleeve is pinned a massive pendant depicting Diana and Acteon. Both pendants, suspended by chains, have a cartouche-shaped frame in which is enacted the classical legend, the human figures and grotesques executed in enamel and gems.

The Queen often gave jewels as a sign of favour and as a symbol of her feelings towards someone; a reciprocal example of this is described in a letter written by a steward of Lord Thomas Heneage (Treasurer of the Royal Household) to Lady Heneage in July 1583:

> I weas yesternyght with Mistress Skydmore to knowe howe her Majestie dyd, who delyveryd me a token from her Majestie to my master. Ytt was a butterflye of mother of perle as I take ytt, with this message, that her Excellencye knowying that her Sanguyne [the Queen's nickname for Heneage] was farre in the colde north countrye where no [butter] flyes weare, dyd send hym that butterflye to playe with, that he myght allowayes remember her that sent ytt, and she herselfe dyd and wolde weare the bodkyn and pendant that he sent her on that eare that shoulde heare nothing that sholde hurte him.[19]

A more obvious and public message was intended by the Queen's use of the image of the phoenix. This mythical bird could renew itself only by burning to death and arising anew from the flames, and thus was a symbol of uniqueness and chastity. In the famous portrait by Hilliard (*70*) Elizabeth wears an enamelled pendant of the phoenix. The motif occurs in many other forms and

70. Queen Elizabeth I. Attr. Nicholas Hilliard, c.*1575.*
(The National Portrait Gallery, London)

can be found on a pendant in the British Museum in which a gold bust of the Queen, surrounded by a wreath of enamelled roses and eglantine, has on its reverse a phoenix in flames under the royal monogram, crown and heavenly rays.

The language of colour was particularly complex. One of the most influential treatises on colour symbolism was Sicile's *Le Blason des Couleurs en Armes, Livrees et Devises*, 1526. It was translated into English by R [ichard] R [obinson] and published in 1583 with the title *A Rare True and Proper Blazon of Coloures and Ensignes Military with theyr Peculiar Signification.* In this book we find that black indicates 'grief and constancy; obscure grey, patience; bright grey, despair; ash, trouble and sadness; yellow, hope, joy, magnaminity; russet, prudence; yellow-red, deception; green, love, joy; blue, amity; turquoise; jealousy; perse, knowledge; red, prowess; vermilion, courage'.

Combinations of colours could convey a specific abstract idea; for example, 'white and green, virtuous youth; white and grey, hope of coming to perfection . . . white and tawny, patience in adversity', and 'incarnate and tawny, misfortune'.[20] An interesting insight into one person's use of colour to express an emotion can be found in the *Autobiography of Thomas Whythorne*, 1576, in which he wrote:

> . . . because I would seem to live in hope, I would go sometimes in garments of russet colour (the which colour signifieth the wearer thereof to have hope). And one time I did wear hops in my hat also; the which when my mistress had espied she in a few scoffing words told me that the wearing of hops did but show that I should hope without that which I hoped for'.[21]

As colours spoke a language of their own, when a lover wore the colour of his mistress he could let it speak for him. In Jonson's play *Cynthia's Revels*, 1601, Amorphus instructs Asotus in this silent language:

> Or, if you can possess your opposite that the green your mistreis wears is her rejoicing or exultation in his service; the yellow, suspicion of his truth, from her height of affection: and that he, greenly credulous, shall withdraw this, in private, and from the abundance of his pocket to displace her jealous conceit steal into his hat the colour whose blueness doth express trueness, shee being nor so affected, you give him the dor. (V.ii.28–35)

Queen Elizabeth told the Spanish ambassador in 1564 that her favourite colours were black and white, as they were symbolic of virginity, and it is a colour combination that was worn by many of her courtiers in deference to her.[22] In the later years of her reign, white was worn universally at court. Don Virginio Orsini observed in 1600 that 'the whole court that day . . . was dressed in white with so much gold and jewels, that it was a marvellous thing. 'The Queen was dressed all in white, with so many pearls, broderies and diamonds that I am amazed how she could carry them.'[23] According to Sicile, white symbolized chastity, humility and faith, and silver purity.

The use of colour as a visual expression of a person's deepest feelings can be found in this poem about a lady whose husband has deserted her. Her grief is stated in her embroidery:

> Give me black silk, that sable suites my hart,
> And yet som white, though white words do deceive,
> No green at all, for youth and I must part,
> Purple and blew, fast love and faith to weare.
> Mayden, no more sleepless Ile goe to bedd,
> Take all away, the work works in my head.[24]

If a man was suffering from the fashionable affliction of melancholy, he could express it by affecting a certain style of dress. The Elizabethans believed in the Renaissance theory of physiology which stated that a person's character, actions and qualities were determined by his humour. A predominance of one of the four humours would make him either choleric, melancholic, sanguine or phlegmatic. Melancholy was the humour most closely linked to genius, and so appealed to anyone with intellectual or artistic pretensions, like the character in Jonson's *Every Man in his Humour* who states: 'I am melancholy myself, divers times, sir, and then do I no more but take pen and paper presently, and overflow you half a score, or a dozen of sonnets at a sitting'.[25]

Thomas Overbury in his *Book of Characters* explains how one can recognize a man

71. Unknown man. Nicholas Hilliard, c.1590. (By courtesy of the Board of Trustees of the Victoria & Albert Museum, London)

who is melancholic because of an unhappy love-life:

> His armes are carelessly used, as if their best use were nothing but embracements. He is untrust and unbuttoned, ungartered not out of carelessness, but care . . . He scocheth time with dancing with his Mistres, taking up of hir glove, and wearing hir feather; he is confinde to hir colour and dares not passe out of the circuit of hir memorie.

His preoccupation with his thoughts is signified by unbuttoned and untied clothes and a tendency to fidget, 'playing with the string of your band, which is a most quaint kind of melancholy'.[26] This preference for a state of undress can be seen in Hilliard's minature of a young man against a background of flames (*71*). He wears a white lawn shirt, the lace falling collar of which is open at the neck, and clasps the cause of his misery – a miniature of his mistress. His inner feelings of passion are symbolized by the background of flames.

A dark hat with a large shady brim was another feature of melancholic dress, and one is worn by the unknown man in Isaac Oliver's miniature in the Royal Collection painted *c.*1595 (*72*). The colours of the doublet, yellow and black, are significant as they symbolize sadness at the departure of a loved one. Ann Clifford recorded in her diary that she wore a black nightgown and yellow waistcoat when her husband went away.[27] The same meaning is attached to the colours in this song from Nashe's *Summer's Last Will and Testament*, 1600:

> Falangtado, Falangtado,
> To weare the black and yellow,
> Falantado, Falantado,
> My mates are gone, I'll follow.[28]

A melancholic and rather surreal motif that occurs in embroidery is an eye shedding tears. It is illustrated in Peacham's *Minerva Britanna* (*73*) with the explanatory text,

72. Unknown man. Isaac Oliver, 1595. (Reproduced by gracious permission of Her Majesty the Queen)

This motif, embroidered in metal thread, can be found on the white satin gauntlet of a glove in the Metropolitan Museum in New York (*74*), and is also found, next to a pierced heart, on a dress trimming in the Victoria & Albert Museum.[29] On the glove the motif is positioned above a pansy (also called love-in-idleness and heartsease). This flower symbolized sadness, for its name is thought to have derived from the French word for thoughts, *pensées*. In *Hamlet*, the mad Ophelia offers a pansy, saying, 'there is pansies, that's for thoughts' (IV.v.177). The flower also features in *A Midsummer Night's Dream* when Oberon directs Puck to pick the flower so that it can be used as a love potion. It was a popular flower with the Elizabethan embroiderer

73. Henry Peacham, Minerva Britanna, *London, 1612.* (By courtesy of the Trustees of the British Museum)

. . . while coldest sorrow fills
My brest by flames, enforce this moisture thence
In Christall floods.

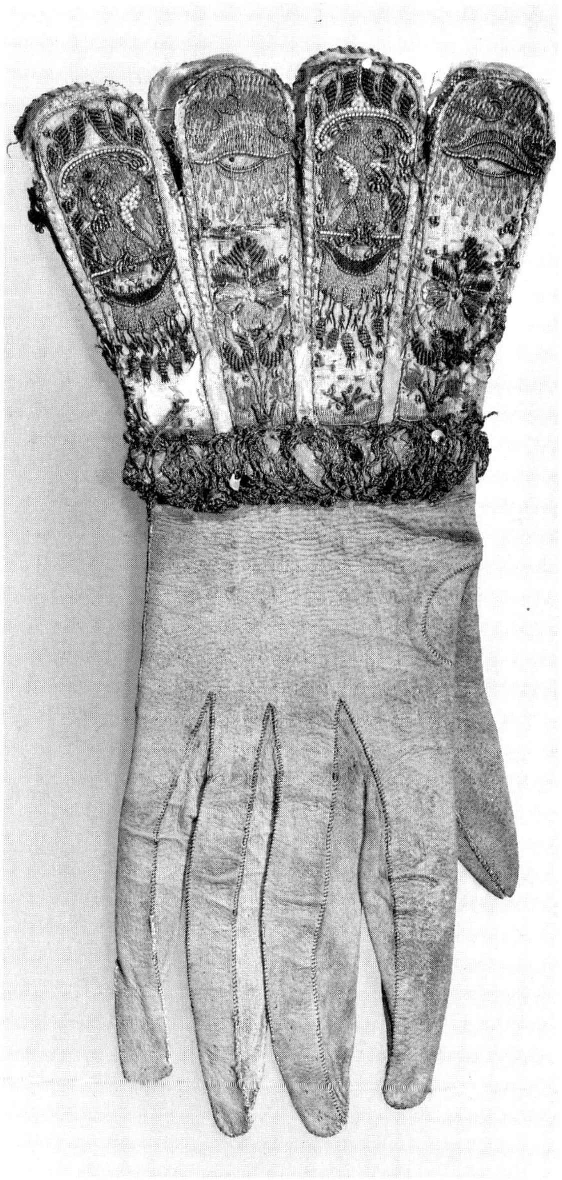

74. Embroidered glove. Silk and metal thread, seed pearls and spangles, 1595–1620. (The Metropolitan Museum of Art, New York, The Gift of Mrs Edward S. Harkness, 1928)

and appeared on many garments presented to Elizabeth. In 1600, for example, she received a 'loose gown of blacke satten embroidered all ouer with roses and pauncies, and a border of aken (oak) leaves roses and pauncies'.[30] As mentioned earlier, the pansy was also an emblem of the Queen's chastity, and that would be the meaning intended in this embroidery.

Another visual indication that a man was in love with his mistress was the wearing of her favours. A selection of these are listed in the play *How a Man May Chuse a Good Wife from a Bad*, 1602, when the hero explains that once he was a melancholic person:

> . . . a busk-point wearer,
> One that did use much bracelets of haire,
> Rings on my fingers, Jewels in mine eares,
> And now and then a wenches Carkenet,
> That had two letters for her name in Pearle:
> Scarves, garters, bands, wrought wastcoats, gold, sticht caps . . .[31]

Gloves, handkerchiefs and ribbons could be placed in the man's hat, and an example of this practice can be seen in Hilliard's portrait of George Clifford, 3rd Earl of Cumberland, who shows that he is the Queen's Champion by wearing her glove pinned to his hat (*96*). Sir Phillip Sidney in *Astrophel and Stella* complains about the superficiality of the court ladies who do not consider that a man can be in love with them if he does not wear their colours:

> Because I breathe not love to every one,
> Nor do not use set colours for to wear,
> Nor nourish special locks of vowed hair . . .
> 'What, he?' say they of me, 'now I dare swear
> He cannot love! No, no, let him alone.'[32]

1585 saw the publication of Samuel Daniel's *The worthy Tract of Paulus Iouius contayning a Discourse of rare intentions both Militarie and Amorous called Imprese.* This book explained the difference between emblems and imprese: 'Emblems are generall conceiptes rather of moral matters than particulare deliberations . . . whether the inuention bee embrodred in garmentes, grauen in stone, enchased in golde, wrought in Arras.' Imprese, or devices, as the Elizabethans called them, should be worn by 'armed men or maskers' at 'Iusts, Turneis, Maskes, or at such like extravagant shewes' and should be 'worne in such places as they best like about their persons: albeit the helmet, the shielde, the Bardes, the borders of the garment, or the brest'.[33]

The most spectacular occasion for the display of imprese was the Accession Day Tilt, when the Queen's knights in elaborate fancy dress jousted for her favour. The entrance of the knights, either on horseback or in pageant cars with their accompanying retinue and torchbearers, was a moment of pure theatre. Each knight would plan his costume very carefully, for its colour and decoration would complement the message embodied by the device on his pasteboard shield. It was important that the device should not be too obscure, as the spectator wanted to show his intellectual superiority by deciphering it; the enjoyment of this feeling of 'wonder and delight' arose from the fact 'that one sees one thing used to express another'.[34]

The shields would be presented to the Queen by the knight's squire, and those judged to be the most successful were afterwards hung in a gallery at Whitehall Palace to be pointed out to visitors. The picturesque appearance of these shields is clearly illustrated in Hilliard's portrait of George Clifford, who stands in his Tilt costume while his shield with its astrological symbols hangs on a tree beside him (*96*). Henry

Peacham's *Minerva Britanna* includes some of the devices that were featured in the Tilts and in the conclusion of the book he described a vision of Elizabeth surrounded by shields:

About her now on every tree
(Wheron full oft she cast her eie)
Hung silver shields, by three and three
With pencil limned curiouslie
Wherein were drawne with skilfull touch
Impresa's and devices rare
Of all her gallant knightes and such
As actors in her conquests were.

Chapter Five

'Each degree has his fashion': *Dress and social status*

DRESS IN THE fifteenth and sixteenth centuries clearly reflected the wearer's class, rank and profession, and to ensure that this state of affairs continued, penalties were imposed on men and women who attempted to dress in a manner above their status. These rules were set out in sumptuary legislation, a series of ten proclamations issued between 1559 and 1597 which sought to define exactly what fabrics, furs and trimmings could be worn by each rank.[1] It seems doubtful whether their stipulations were always enforced, for as Stubbes observed in 1583: '. . . now there is such a confuse mingle mangle of apparell in Ailgna (England) . . . that it is verie hard to knowe who is noble, who is worshipfull, who is a gentleman, who is not'.[2] He believed, as did the government, that 'every man should be compelled to weare apparell according to his degree, estate and condition'[3] so that a general decorum could be observed in a society whose relationships were experiencing an 'increasing degree of mobility'.[4] The main cause of this social mobility was the rise of the gentry class with their increased spending power and desire for imported goods, and the slow erosion of the nobility's position of power and supremacy in the country.

A sumptuary law of 1566 attempted to check this development by restating the division of the population into nine distinct categories with a detailed description of what each category was permitted to wear. This statute was thought to be necessary because of the 'disorder and confusion of the degrees of all estates'.[5] The first category consisted of Dukes, Marquises, Earls and barons; the second of sons of barons, knights and those with an income of no less that £200 per year; the third men with an income of no less than £100 per year; the fourth those with an income of £40 per year; the fifth £20 per year; the sixth £5 per year; the seventh servingmen taking wages, yeomen taking wages, and those with a freehold worth forty shillings a year; the eighth group husbandmen, and at the bottom were servingmen. If anyone so categorized wore clothing defined as beyond their status, then they were liable to have their clothes impounded and be fined three shillings and fourpence for each offence committed.

The legislation also tried to check the flood of imported fabrics into England and to protect the native cloth industry by stating that the only foreign fabric that those in group six could wear in their doublets and jackets was camlet, while those belonging to group seven could not wear a bonnet or shirtband 'made out of the realm of England and Wales'. Control of the wearing of silk, satin, damask and velvet was attempted, but it was virtually impossible to enforce. All those in category three were allowed to wear velvet for 'sleeveless jackets, doublets, coifs and partlets and purses', but could not use satin, damask, silk and taffeta for outer garments. Petticoats of velvet, tufted taffeta and satin were supposed to be worn only by the wives of barons, knights and councillors, ladies of the Privy Chamber and the Maids of Honour. One clue to the wholesale disregard of this legislation was that the regulations do not appear to have been enforced with any severity. Emmison found in exhaustive studies of the records of Essex only one case of someone being fined for non-compliance[6] and Sir John Harrington even wrote a poem about the ineffectiveness of the law against 'excesse in womans apparel':

> Our zealous preachers that would pride repress,
> Complain against Apparells great excess,
> For though the laws against yt are express,
> Each lady like a Queen herself doth dress,
> A merchaunts wife like to a baroness[2]

Sumptuary legislation also tried to regulate the more exaggerated fashions and to lay down guidelines for the production of clothes. In 1562 a statute was passed 'for the reformation of the use of monstrous and outrageous greatness of hose'. It forbade any tailor or hosier to use more than a yard and a half or at the most a yard and three-quarters of cloth for the outside of the hose. Apart from a linen cloth lining there was to be only one other lining, which should not be loose or stuffed, but to lie just under the legs'.[8] This ruling proved as ineffectual as the attempted control of the size of ruffs; double ruffs were not permitted at the neck and wrists, only single ruffs being allowed, 'and the singleness to be used in a due and mean sort, as was orderly and comely used before the coming in of the outrageous and double ruffs which now of late are crept in'.[9] More practically, the length of weapons was regulated in this statute, with no sword or rapier to have a blade more than 'one yard and a quarter'.[10]

Legislation passed in 1571 to benefit the English capmakers required that every person above seven years of age should wear on Sabbath and Holy Days a 'cap of wool knit thicked and dressed in England . . . upon pain to forfeit for every day not wearing, three shillings fourpence'.[11] Maids, ladies, gentlewomen, noble personages and every lord, knight and gentleman of twenty marks' land were exempted. These so-called 'statute caps' were worn by citizens and apprentices for a time, but the law was not enforced and was finally abandoned in 1597. The attire of the London apprentices was carefully regulated by an ordinance of 1582 which stated that 'no apprentice whatsoever shall wear apparel but what he received from his master'. The clothing that he would have received during the reign of Queen Mary was described by Stow:

> all apprentices in London wore blew cloakes in the Summer and in the Winter blew gownes . . . it was not lawful . . . to wear their gownes lower than to the calves of their legges . . . their breeches and stockings were usually of white broad cloth . . . they also wore flat caps.[12]

The 1582 proclamation stated that doublet and breeches should be of the same material, that neither garment should be decorated, and that they should be worn with a plain coat, cloth gown or cloak. Hose or stockings had to be either white-blue or murrey (mulberry colour).

Regulations were strictly applied to the dress worn by students at Oxford and Cambridge University. When the Earl of Leicester was made Chancellor of Oxford in 1564, he forbade both seniors and juniors to wear doublets of a light colour such as white, green or yellow. In 1578 a complaint was made that Cambridge students were wearing hose of 'unseemly greatness', and they were fined sixpence, and eightpence if they walked through the town without a suitable gown and hood. In 1614 Sir Thomas Overbury in his *Book of Characters* drew a distinction between the dress of an Inn of Court man and that of a university student. The latter, being poorer, 'thinkes himself as fine when he is in a clean bande, and a new pair of shoes, as any courtier doeth when he is first in a new fashion'. He is looked down on by the Inn of Court man who wears an expensive beaver hat and silk stockings and 'laughs at every man whose band sits not a faire shoo-tye, and . . . is ashamed to be seene in any mans companie that wears not his clothes well . . . and his chiefest prayer is, that his revenues may hold out for taffata cloakes in the summer, and velvet in the winter'.[13]

Livery was a special dress or uniform worn by male servants belonging to a large household, or by members of the City companies. A bright blue livery was the usual colour, but it could also be made in grey, russet or tawny. The connexion of blue with servitude ensured that it was a colour which gentlemen never wore, and it is frequently mentioned in this context by contemporary dramatists. A summer and a winter livery formed part of the wages for every servant living in a noble household, such as the broadcloth livery mentioned in the play *Tu Quoque*; 'his colours, they are according to the seasons; in the summer he is apparelled like the heauens in blew, the winter, like the earth in freese'.[14] This system of using blue russet in the summer and the heavier dark-coloured frieze in winter was quite usual.

The most common livery was broadcloth trunk hose and coat, with the badge or 'cognizance' of the household embroidered on the left sleeve. When the noblemen and their retainers were all gathered at court in their brilliantly coloured liveries it made, as Harrison put it, 'a goodlie sight . . . which doth yeeld the contemplation of a noble varietie unto the beholder, much like to the shew of the peacockes taile in the full beautie, or some meadow garnished with infinite kinds and diversitie of pleasant floures'.[15]

It was considered essential for a nobleman to be accompanied by a large number of liveried attendants when making a public appearance. The Earl of Oxford, renowned for his extravagance, arrived in London in 1570 with 'eighty gentlemen in a livery of Reading tawny and chains about their necks, before him one hundred tall yeomen in the like livery to follow him, without chains, but all having his cognizance of the Blue Boar embroidered on their left shoulder'.[16] The Duke of Rutland had peacocks embroidered on the livery of his servants; the gentlemen had the motif embroidered on a velvet ground at a cost of six shillings each, whereas the yeomen had a satin ground costing five shillings each.[17] Sumptuary legislation prevented servants from wearing silk, so an amendment was passed in 1597 allowing the Queen's servants, noblemen's servants and gentlemen's servants to wear 'badges and cognizances or other ornamentes of velvet and silk' on their livery coats and cloaks. Servants in smaller households also received clothing as part of their wages. John Dee, for example, noted in his diary on 29 September 1595 that 'Margery Stubble of Hounslow, our dry nurse, entered into the yere of her service beginning on Michelmas Day, and is to have £3 her yeres wages and a gown cloth of russet'.[18]

The provision of biannual liveries entailed a large financial outlay. In March 1576 Roger North, second Baron North of Kirtling, spent £16 3s. on 40 yards of tawny cloth and gave each man ten shillings to buy a coat. In 1578, when the Queen visited him at Kirtling, £23 3s. 8d was spent on

75. Member of the House of Lords, a Knight of the Garter and a Yeoman of the Guard, from Lucas de Heere's Beschrijving der Britische Eilanden, c.*1570.* (By courtesy of the Trustees of the British Museum)

tawny cloth and £9 on coats.[19] Philip Gawdy was responsible for buying the fabric, buttons and trimming for his family livery, and whilst he was staying in London in 1599 he wrote to his brother to let him know how he was progressing:

> I did think you wolde make hast to have all your lyveryes done out of hande, and therefore I have sent you downe the rest of the buttons which come to fourskore and one dozen which makethe up iust sixskore. I have sent besydes fyue dosen, which I wolde have delyuered to button up for my man's cloke. I have sent besydes 26 yardes of the lace which wayeth iust $5\frac{1}{2}$ ounces so that all the lace together commethe to $24\frac{1}{2}$ ounces. I have sowed them within a shepeskin.[20]

A large and important allocation of the Great Wardrobe expenditure was the distribution each year of a winter livery and a more costly summer livery to all members of the Royal Household. The summer livery for the Yeomen of the Guard has survived in the dress of the Wardens of the Tower of London (Beefeaters). It consisted of a red cloth tunic with a puffed upper sleeve, the back and front of the garment embroidered with gold thread and spangles in a design comprising the initials of the monarch, a rose and a crown (*75*), paned trunk hose and a court bonnet. Their appearance was described by Breuning von Buchenbach when he visited the English court in 1595, 'The Queen's guards who are always attired in red coats with black velvet facings, wear on their breasts and backs roses and the name of her Majesty'.[21] In August 1597, red cloth for summer liveries for the Queen's Yeomen of the Guard and others cost £220 6d., the embroiderer was paid £88 9s. $4\frac{1}{2}$d., and the gold and silver spangles amounted to £401 16s. 2d.[22]

The amount of material and fur given to the officers and staff of the various standing offices was commensurate with their status. The Clerk of the Wardrobe, being a fairly lowly person, received four yards of puke (a woollen textile) for his gown, whereas the Lord Chamberlain as Head of the Household received the highest entitlement of fourteen yards of velvet for his gown.[23] The Queen's dwarf, Thomasina, was not neglected; her livery for 1597 was a 'high-bodied gowne of drake-colour velvet . . . stomacher of white satten cut and lined with sarcenet'.[24]

Woodcuts in George Turbervile's *The Book of Falconrie* and *The noble arte of Venerie or Hunting* contain information about the dress worn by the Queen's grooms, cook, butler and falconer. The liveried attendant walking beside her horse (*76*) wears exaggerated paned trunk hose

76. Illustration from George Turbervile's The noble arte of Venerie or Hunting, *1575.* (By courtesy of the Trustees of the British Museum)

1. Portrait of a lady, possibly of the Wentworth family.
Hans Eworth, 1565-8. (The Tate Gallery, London)

2. Mary Denton. George Gower, 1573.
(York City Art Gallery)

MARY
COVNTESs. RIVERS.

4. Mary Fitton (?). Unknown artist, c. 1600. ***(The Weiss Gallery, London)***

5. Robert Dudley, Earl of Leicester. Unknown artist, c. 1577. *(The National Portrait Gallery, London)*

6. Henry Herbert, 2nd Earl of Pembroke. Unknown artist, c. 1590. *(The National Museum of Wales)*

7. Robert Devereux, 2nd Earl of Essex. William Segar, 1590. *(The National Gallery of Ireland, Dublin)*

8. Embroidered jacket, coloured silks and plaited gold braid on linen, *c.* 1600-1625. *(The Burrell Collection, Glasgow Museums and Art Galleries)*

which narrow into the knee, with the royal badge embroidered on the back and the front of his doublet. The falconer, a higher-ranking servant, is allowed to wear a plumed hat with his more fashionable doublet and hose; a hawk rests on his tasselled glove.

When a master craftsman or trader joined the London company which represented his particular skill he would wear its livery at the regular fraternal meetings. Livery was of such symbolic importance that the term for attaining membership was 'to be clothed'. In some companies only the wealthier members could wear the full outfit which comprised a distinctly coloured hood, the badge of the company, a coat or surcoat and a gown for purely ceremonial occasions. The hood was not a functional garment and hung behind, prevented from falling off by a long streamer held in front. This streamer was a vestigial remnant of the fifteenth-century liripipe, a tail which extended from the pointed cowl of the medieval hood.

Physicians, surgeons, teachers and other professional men wore long gowns over their normal fashionable dress and, in the case of the medical profession, a flat bonnet over a coif (*77*). In a woodcut (*78*) from Bateman's *Crystal Glass of Christian Reformation*, 1569, the schoolboys create havoc while the teacher, in a flat cap and long fur-lined gown, sleeps. The uniform of the judiciary was quite distinctive and consisted of a long, girdled robe, a hood, coif and mantle. The latter, being a symbol of magisterial authority, was fastened on the right shoulder to hang just above the underlying robe. By 1600 the mantle was turned back towards the left shoulder to reveal the inner lining, which in winter was miniver and in summer taffeta or sarcenet.[25]

77. William Bullein. Frontispiece from Bullein's Bulwarke of Defence against all Sickness, *1566.* (By courtesy of the Trustees of the British Museum)

The clothing worn by all classes of country people was easily recognizable and was often the subject of scathing comment in fashionable circles. At the bottom of the social scale was the labourer, a landless wage earner, who worked on someone else's land for a fixed rate. Above him was the husbandman, who was either a tenant farmer or small copyholder (a tenant of land belonging to a manor), and so was neither a daily wage earner like the labourer nor a yearly wage earner like the yeoman. The chief basis for yeoman status was the holding of free land to the annual value of forty shillings; above the yeomen was the gentry.

78. Illustration from Stephen Bateman's A Christall Glass of Christian Reformation, *1569.* (By courtesy of the Trustees of the British Museum)

Differentiation between these groups was maintained by sumptuary legislation, though the disparity between the dress worn by the wives and daughters of well-to-do yeomen and that worn by the gentry had narrowed somewhat by the end of Elizabeth's reign. Country people tended to be more conservative in their dress and so there was less interest in innovation in fashion than amongst the burghers and professional people.

The easily recognizable dress worn by a countryman when he visited London marked him out as an easy prey for the 'connie-catcher', the Elizabethan equivalent of a con-man. Robert Greene in his pamphlet *A notable discovery of coosnage now daily practised by sundry lewd persons, called connie-biters*, 1591, describes how they lay in wait for a 'plain country fellow well and cleanly apparelled either in a coat of homespun russet or of frieze as the time requires, and a side pouch at his side'.[26] The yeoman's wife was expected to make her own and her family's clothes from home-grown wool and flax, but her best dress and her husband's best suit were sometimes made by a local tailor. As an industrious and thrifty housewife, she had to mend and patch clothes to make them last for as long as possible. The contrast between the home-spun cloth breeches worn by a yeoman and the velvet breeches of a gentleman was used by Francis Thynne in his *The debate between pride and lowliness*, 1570, to symbolize the different values embraced by each class; both wore trunk hose, but the poor countryman's sensible hose were made of cloth that exactly corresponded with the 1562 statute:

> These last were but cloth, withouten pride,
> An stitche, ne gard upon them was to see.
> Of cloth (I say) both upper and neather,
> Paned, and single lyned next to the thie;
> Light for the were, meete for al sort of weather.

The rich man, on the other hand, 'wore . . . velvet very fine',

79. Frontispiece from Robert Greene's A Quip for an Upstart Courtier, *1592.* (By courtesy of the Trustees of the British Museum)

80. Illustration from M. van Meer's Album Amicorum, *1614.* (Edinburgh University Library)

> The neather stockes of pure Grenado silke,
> . . . And with satten very costly lined,
> Embrodred according to the guise,
> With golden lace full craftely engined'.[27]

The contrast between the appearance of the two men is also employed in the frontispiece to Robert Green's pamphlet, *Quips for an Upstart Courtier*, 1592 (*79*).

The simple functional dress worn by a husbandman at work is described by Thynne in the same poem:

> Full sunburnt was his forehead and his snoute.
> A man aboute a fiftie yeeres of age:
> Of Kendall very coarse his coate was made . . .
> Upon his grydle hong a rustye blade.
> Full simple was thereof both haft and sheath;
> A strawen hatte he had upon his head,
> The which his chinne was fastened underneath
> A payre of startuppes had he on his feete,
> That lased were up to the small of the legge;
> Homelie they were, and easier than meete,
> And in their soles full many a wooden pegge.
> He had a shyrt of canvas hard and tough,
> Of which the band and ruffes, were both of one.[28]

This description is confirmed in a sketch of a countryman made by Michael Van Meer when he visited London in 1614 (*80*). The man wears a loose, simple tunic, baggy

81. Detail from map by J. Hoefnagel, published in Braun and Hogenberg's Civitates Orbis Terrarum, *1574.* (By courtesy of the Trustees of the British Museum)

leggings and a pouch fastened to his waist. The clothes worn by his wife are almost identical to those of two countrywomen bringing their wares to market, included in a line of figures at the foot of a view of Nonsuch Palace engraved by Hoefnagel and published in Braun and Hogenberg's *Civitates Orbis Terrarum*, 1574 (*81*). The standing figure with a basket wears a bodice and a skirt, neck-kerchief over the shoulders, long apron, wide-brimmed hat, small neck ruff and chin-clout. The chin-clout was a large square of material folded diagonally and worn over chin and mouth to keep out any dust encountered on the long journey to market. The first lady in the line of figures (captioned *Englishwoman*) wears a plain closed gown, small ruff, cap and coif. This is in sharp contrast to the noble lady at the end of the line with her elegant closed gown with fur revers and guards, rich underskirt, partlet, ruff and bowler-style hat topped with a bunch of feathers. The fourth woman wears a more subdued version of this outfit with a high-crowned hat. The tall hat worn over an undercap accords with Platter's description of the headwear of English burgher-women; 'high hats covered with velvet or silk'.[29] The second and third women are

82. Illustration from Stephen Bateman's A Christall Glass of Christian Reformation, *1569.* (By courtesy of the Trustees of the British Museum)

labelled *merchant's wives*, the second being apparently the richer of the two, for she holds a tasselled scarf in one hand and a pomander suspended from her girdle in the other, while the woman next to her carries a wicker basket under her arm and wears an apron tied over her skirt. This combination of accessories suggests that she is a shop-keeper, whereas her companion is a lady of leisure.

Labourers, whether they worked in town or country, wore a loose belted garment buttoned across the chest with an open knee-length skirt. Over this could be worn a jacket, but if this was of the looser variety it was called a coat. The upper garment would be worn with loose breeches, coarse stockings or canvas leggings buskined with leather or strips of cloth. Labourers could also wear a modified version of trunk hose, as does the man in fig. *82* under a rather ragged apron. Michael van Meer illustrated the dress worn by a London carter and a Smithfield porter (*83*). The carter has a sheepskin jacket over a doublet and breeches and the porter, carrying a wicker basket of meat on his back, wears a slightly pointed cap, a linen shirt, breeches belted at the waist, loose leggings and flat shoes. In a watercolour drawing from the *Album*

83. Illustration from M. van Meer's Album Amicorum, *1614.* (Edinburgh University Library)

84. Illustration from Album Amicorum *of Frederick of Botnia, c.1616–18.* (By courtesy of the Trustees of the British Museum)

Amicorum of Frederick of Botnia, *c.*1616–18 we see another distinctive sight of Elizabethan London (*84*). The watercarrier used his wooden container to transport water from the Thames and conduits into people's homes. Here he is represented as a blind man led by his dog. His protective overgarment, a black smock, is also included in earlier illustrations.

Visitors to England in the sixteenth and early seventeenth centuries were intrigued by the distinctive dress worn by members of the traditional English institutions, and were particularly impressed by the spectacle and careful delineation of status which any procession in London afforded. Fortunately a few visual and written accounts of their observations have survived, as it was the custom for students travelling around Europe to ask any eminent people that they encountered to sign their names and write a motto in an early form of autograph album called an *Album Amicorum.*[30] These inscriptions were interspersed with illustrations of people wearing unusual dress. Georg von Holzschuher's album includes part of the procession of the Lord and Lady Mayoress of London (*85*). Since the Lord Mayor was a dignitary unique to London, the splendour of his costume and that of his retinue ensured that a procession would be an event which no visitor would want to miss. The Lord Mayor is shown on horseback clad in his robes, described by Thomas Platter in 1599 as, 'black with a velvet hat' and 'a red coat lined with fur'. He is preceded by a swordbearer who, according to Platter, carries a 'red sword with yellow stripes, bared and vertical'; on his head is 'a white hat'.[31] Another visitor, von Kiechel, gave us a little more information about this curious hat when he observed the scene in 1585; it was a 'broad high cap open at the top' and made of miniver. Behind the Mayor is the City Remembrancer in a black gown. Von Kiechel records that the throng of people watching the procession was so dense that stewards were obliged to squirt water at the crowd to clear a pathway.[32]

Lucas de Heere, a Flemish artist who stayed in England between 1566 and 1571, illustrated the dress of the English, Scots and Irish of all classes. Fig. *75* is taken from his *Beschrijving der Britische Eilanden* and shows, from left to right, a member of Parliament, a Knight of the Garter, and a Yeoman of the Guard. The Order of the Garter was the most exclusive Order in England, being limited to 26 men chosen by the Queen herself. Buchenbach noted in 1595 that they wore a long red velvet gown lined with white silk and over it a brown velvet cloak, the curious hood of which was a relic from the medieval period and an instance of the way that professional, academic and ceremonial dress frequently fossilizes an earlier fashion.[33] The oldest complete set of insignia of the Order, originally belonging to the Earl of Northampton who was made a Knight in 1628, is now in the British Museum. It consists of three items, the largest being the collar of the Order which is made of enamelled gold roses within garters alternating with gold knots. From this chain hangs the Great George (*32*), an enamelled gold pendant of St George and his horse trampling the dragon. The lesser George would be worn when 'full dress' was not required (*46*, colour pls 5, 6). The third item in the set is the garter itself, worn below the left knee and made of velvet with the motto *Honi soit qui mal y pense* enamelled across it.

Elevation in status for an Elizabethan was usually recorded by having a portrait painted, for which event the acquisition of new clothes was essential. When Simon Forman married in 1599 he spend £50 on new clothes for himself and his wife, and they then both sat for portraits.[34] If the sitter held a distinguished office, the artist would give the symbols of that office a prominent place in the portrait. Nicholas Bacon, Keeper of the Great Seal and Lord

85. Illustration from Album Amicorum *of Georg von Holzschuher, c.1623.* (By courtesy of the Trustees of the British Museum)

1579
ÆTATIS SVÆ 68
MEDIOCRIA FIRMA

86. Sir Nicholas Bacon. Unknown artist, 1579. (The National Portrait Gallery, London)

Chancellor, sat for a portrait by an unknown artist in 1579 (*86*) wearing professional headgear – a flat bonnet over a black skullcap – fur-trimmed doublet and a black gown. The Chancellor's Burse or Purse for the Great Seal (embroidered with the Royal Arms and initials) has been placed in the bottom right-hand corner so that it is clear which office Bacon held. An almost identical purse for the Great Seal, with the Royal Arms and the initials ER embroidered on it, measuring 14 × 11 inches and embroidered in gold and silver, is in a private collection. This particular purse is illustrated in G.W. Digby's *Elizabethan Embroidery* (Faber & Faber, 1963), plate 40.

Marriage and family portraits were one expression of a consuming interest in genealogy and the desire to record the social rank attained by the family. Funeral processions and funerary monuments were also designed with this purpose in mind, an attitude that is made plain in John Weever's *Ancient Funeral Monuments*: '. . . sepulchres should be made according to the qualities and degree of the person deceased, that by the tombe might bee discerned of what ranke he was living'.[35] The funeral itself was arranged so that it was in accordance with the deceased's status, and this expectation is expressed in a yeoman's will of 1610, 'I will that I shall have a buriall fitt and decent for my degree'.[36] An Elizabethan funeral commenced with a formal and carefully organized procession, with the status of every person in the entourage delineated by the dress that he or she wore. The order of procession was laid down by the College of Arms, and representations of the heraldic devices of the deceased (if he or she came from an arms-bearing family) were given a prominent place. The chief mourners wore a mourning hood over their heads and a mourning gown, with the amount of material governed by rank. The bearers of the coffin were usually men of the yeoman class and because they were far down the social scale wore black coats. A Countess, on the other hand, would wear the distinctive mourning costume of mantle with train, surcoat with front train folded over girdle, open mourning hood and barbe (white bib of pleated linen worn around the chin). Other mourners in the procession and the entire staff of the household would be supplied with black gowns with hoods on the left shoulder in the style of Garter and livery dress. If the deceased was head of a large household the provision of black cloth for servants and members of the family could be extremely expensive.

Hentzner's comment in 1598 that the English were 'lovers of show' is typical of most visitors' reactions after a stay in London. The equation of strength and power with ostentatious display was seen at Court, in the City and in the country, and it gave rise to many ceremonial occasions at which the rigid hierarchical system was clearly shown in the style of dress adopted by each participant. The concept that 'each degree has his fashion' was one of the underlying principles in society, and the increased movement between social goups was felt to be a threat to society's stability and accepted order. This was a fear that proved justified when, during the reign of Charles I, traditional values were questioned, examined and finally rejected.

Chapter Six

'Straunge fantastick habit'

festive dress

THOMAS NASHE, WRITING in 1593, described the fashionable Englishman as 'the ape of all nation's superfluities, the continual Masquer of outlandish habilements'.[1] The use of the word 'masque' to describe contemporary fashion is an illuminating one, as Nashe evidently felt that fashionable dress had become so extreme that it resembled the exotic costumes that would be worn in a masque and as such was quite unsuitable for normal everyday life. There was a clear division between the two, with fancy dress being worn only on special festive occasions like masques, pageants and tournaments. Much attention was given to the design of costumes worn at these events. Francis Bacon's essay *Of Masques and Triumphs* must have been of great help to would-be participants, as it offers advice on how to design effective masque dress, 'Let the suits of the masquers be graceful, and such as become the person when the vizars are off: not after examples of known attires; Turks, soldiers, mariners and the like'.[2].

To find an unusual costume, an Elizabethan would consult an illustrated book of national dress. An increased interest in the costume and customs of foreign countries had stimulated a demand for these books which showed in detail the costumes worn in every country of the known world. The wide circulation enjoyed by the books meant that there was an awareness of costume and its national characteristics that had not previously been possible. The most popular sourcebook for ideas was Boissard's *Habitus Variarum Orbis Gentium*, 1587.[3] This was used for two masque headdresses shown in the present work (*92*, *93*), and Captain Thomas Lee chose to have himself depicted as an Irish soldier in a portrait of 1594 (*87*). He was the nephew of Sir Henry Lee (*88*) and had served for some time in Ireland. For his portrait he wore an idealized version of the dress of an Irishman, as illustrated in Boissard's book. This rather curious costume, comprising a tucked-up shirt and bare legs, was worn by Irish soldiers so that they could make their way through the watery bogs of Ireland with greater ease. Lee's embroidered shirt and lace falling collar would have been very costly and was quite unlike the more serviceable type that an Irish infantryman would have worn.

87. Thomas Lee. Marcus Gheeraerts, 1594. The Tate Gallery, London

Facere et pati Fortia
Henry Lee of Ireland

88. Sir Henry Lee. Antonio Mor, 1568. (The National Portrait Gallery, London)

Boissard also compiled a book of masque costume designs entitled *Mascarades Recueilles*, 1597, and these display his knowledge of historical dress, as many of the costumes are in the International Gothic style (*c.*1390–1430). In fig. 89, the lady wears a gown with characteristically medieval dagged hanging sleeves. The high waistline of the gown, the exotic headdress with its billowing veil and the absence of a farthingale combine to create an effect which has nothing in common with prevailing fashion and so is eminently suitable for a masque costume.

The masque, one of the most popular of English court entertainments, had origi-

89. 'Qui Genio Indulgens' from J. Boissard's Mascarades recueilles, *1597.* (By courtesy of the Trustees of the British Museum)

nated in Italy and was first mentioned in England in 1512. 'The kyng with ten others were disguised, after the manner of Italie, called a maske, a thyng not seen afore in Englande, they were appareled in garmentes long and brode wrought all with gold, with visers and cappes of gold'.[4] It was usual to perform a masque at the end of a banquet and, after a show of verses, singing and dancing, invite the assembled company to join in a formal dance.

Production of a court masque was the responsibility of the Master of Revels, who gave orders to another permanent official to

> obtain stuffs from mercers or from the Wardrobe itself; ornaments from the Jewel House and Mint; to engage architects, carpenters, painters, tailors and embroiderers; to superintend the actual performances in the banqueting-hall or the Tilt-yard, and attempt to preserve the costly and elaborate pageants from the rifling of guests; to have custody of the dresses, visors and properties.[5]

A large ancillary staff was required to make the enormous number of props and costumes required during the festive season (from Christmas to Twelfth Night). This limited season often caused the team of tailors, painters and property-makers to work day and night. A patent dated 24 December 1581 authorized the Master of Revels to employ at 'competent wages . . . as many painters, imbroderers, taylors, haberdashers . . . armourers . . . feathermakers and all other property makers and conninge artificers and labourers whatsoever . . . as he thought necessary'.[6]

Performances were generally held in the Hall or Great Chamber of the palace currently occupied by the Queen, but if the occasion was exceptionally important a temporary structure was erected. One such, built in Whitehall in 1581, was not pulled down until 1606, and in its place still stands Inigo Jones's magnificent Banqueting House. The earlier building was constructed in three months and three days at a cost of £1,744 19s. Its extraordinary interior was lined with canvas to look like stone, the walls were set with 'two hundred ninetie and two lights of glass', and the canvas ceiling was painted with flowers, fruits, clouds, stars and sunbeams all studded with spangles.[7]

An important consideration in the design of costumes that would be seen in such a setting was that they should look effective in candlelight, since performances were always at night. Francis Bacon, in his essay *Of masques and triumphs*, 1594, gave some advice about the choice of colours and trimmings: 'The colours that shew best by candlelight, are white, carnation and a kind of sea-water-greene; and oes, or spangs, as they are of no great cost, so they are of most glory. As for rich embroidery, it is lost, and not discerned'.[8]

There are frequent references in the Office of Revels accounts to costumes made of 'tynsell'. This was especially suitable as it was a silk material interwoven with gold or silver thread to give a glittering surface, and was cheaper than cloth of gold. The trimmings, gold tassels, gilt bells, silver and gold lace, and a wide variety of fringing, gave the costumes a sparkling and highly ornamented surface. There are many references in the accounts to makers of 'spangs' (sequins) and 'bugles' (beads). Typically, in the 1572/3 accounts there is an entry of payment to John Bettes and his wife for 'one day and night's work spangling of the heedpeeces'.[9]

It is possible to form an idea of the appearance of Elizabethan masque dress by studying the Office of Revels manuscripts, as they contain detailed information about the fabrics and trimmings ordered for a few of the performances. Visual evidence is provided by a series of paintings of ladies who are wearing unusual dress which cannot be identified with normal fashionable dress and it becomes evident that Continental masque design had made some impression on the English before the death of Queen Elizabeth.

A 'mask of Amasones' was performed at Richmond Palace in 1579 in the presence of the Queen and the French ambassador, and as it was an event of some significance the costumes are described in great detail. Each of the six ladies involved wore 'Armore compleate parcell gilte' (partially gilded) with silver helmets, also partially gilded. The helmets were worn over long silk wigs for which a silkman used two and a quarter pounds of silk. Their outer skirts were made from crimson cloth of gold with a serrated hem, and the surface was covered with silver lace and fringing, gold tassels and knobs and 'broches of golde plated upon the skirt with plates of silver lawne'. This skirt appears to have been looped over an underskirt of white silver tinsel fringed with gold. On their legs they wore orange velvet buskins and they carried 'antick' shields and staves.[10]

Long blonde wigs are worn by the lady masquers in a detail from the 'Life of Sir Henry Unton', *c.*1596 (*90*). This unique painting in the National Portrait Gallery[11] shows a masque being performed in a private house. The procession is led by the goddess Diana who is identified by the crescent moon in her headdress and her bow and arrow. She is preceded by Mercury, messenger of the gods and the presenter of the masque; he gives Lady Unton a piece of paper which will explain the device being enacted. Behind Diana are six pairs of maidens who carry bows and garlands. They wear circlets of flowers on their heads and grey-green bodices with white trailing skirts patterned with red flowers, which are worn without farthingales. Their faces are obscured by red masks and these will not be removed until the performance has been completed. Alternating with the maidens are pairs of children, dressed as black and white Cupids, who perform the essential role of torchbearers. Masks were usually made of velvet and it appears that they could be quite elaborate, as we know that the artist 'Haunce Eottes' (probably Hans Eworth) designed 'patternes for maskes' for the 1573/4 season at Court.[12]

The costume worn by these masquers and the Amazons bears little resemblance to contemporary Italian theatrical dress, this being a mixture of classical drapery and exuberant Renaissance decoration. Since women were not allowed to take part in formal public theatre, they were enthusiastic participants in private theatrical events and public festivals, in which they played the parts of allegorical and mythological figures. At an Italian *intermezzo* (a form of pantomime which included madrigals and some dancing) the ladies would be dressed as nymphs, their costume dictated by the Renaissance conception of classical dress. A detailed description of this type of dress can be found in Leone de 'Sommi's *Quattro dialoghi in materia di rappresentazione sceniche*, written between 1565 and 1566 at the court of the Duke of Mantua.[13] The principal garment was a loose lawn *camicia* or chemise which was covered with a profusion of rich decoration, leaving only the sleeves and the bottom part of the skirt visible. Over the *camicia* was placed a mantle worn asymmetrically over one

90. Detail from the Life of Sir Henry Unton. Unknown artist, c.*1596.* (The National Portrait Gallery, London)

shoulder. The hair should be blonde and worn loose with a garland or filet tied across the head. Male audiences much appreciated the short clinging skirts, which were a cause of great excitement when they first appeared at the French court in 1584.

Bernardo Buontalenti's design of a nymph's costume for an *intermezzo* performed in 1589 is preserved in the Print Room of the Victoria & Albert Museum (*91*). His sophisticated design has been executed in a spirited Mannerist style that anticipates Inigo Jones' designs of almost two decades later. The skirts of the *camicia* are soft and graceful, showing the outline of the legs. Both ladies wear a complex arrangement of decorated layers which are loosely based on Roman armour. Their hair is elaborately braided with pearls and jewellery, and one lady wears a feathered plume. A description of an Amazon lady that occurs in Sir Philip Sidney's *Arcadia*, published 1590, corresponds so closely with de Sommi's description and Buontalenti's drawing that it seems as if he is remember-

91. Design for a nymph's costume by Bernardo Buontalenti, 1589. (By courtesy of the Board of Trustees of the Victoria & Albert Museum, London)

ing theatrical dress that he saw in Italy. Her chemise is 'cut after a fashion, that though the length of it reached her ankles, yet in her going one might sometimes discerne the smal of her leg'.[14] She also wears a mantle fastened on one shoulder and a blue satin doublet covered with plates of gold and precious stones – presumably this was the Renaissance version of the Roman *lorica* or breastplace, a standard part of allegorical and mythological costume.

The year 1594 saw a masque at the Scottish court which for the first time contained a reference to classical dress. Rowland Whyte, in a letter to Sir Robert Sidney, described their costume: three ladies wore 'argentine saten' and three others crimson satin, and all six garments were 'enriched with tongue and tinsel of pure gold and silver. Every one of them having a crowne or garland on their heads very richly decked with feathers, perles and jewels upon their loose hair in antica forma'.[15] A conversation in Jonson's play *Cynthia's Revels*, 1601 makes it plain that prints of Italian theatre costume were circulating in England. In this exchange the two ladies are discussing how to wear their hair for that evening's masque:

> PHILAUTIA: Ay, good Phantaste: What! have you changed your head-tire?
> PHANTASTE: Yes, faith, the other was so near the common, it had no extraordinary grace; besides, I had worn it almost a day, in good troth.
> PHILAUTIA: I'll be sworn, this is most excellent for the device, and rare; 'tis after the Italian print we look'd on t'other night'. (II.i.64–71)

The first reference to a mantle occurs in a letter dated 1600 from Rowland Whyte to Sir Robert Sidney, in which he describes a masque that took place at the wedding of one of Elizabeth's maids-of-honour, Ann Russell, who married Lord Herbert. The masque was performed at the house of the bride's mother in the presence of the Queen:

> They have a straunge daunce newly invented their attire is this: each hath a skirt of cloth of silver, a rich waistcoat wrought with silkes and gold and silver, a mantell of carnacion taffeta cast under the arme and their haire loose about their shoulders curiously knotted and interlaced.[16]

92. The 'Rainbow' portrait of Queen Elizabeth I. Attr. Marcus Gheeraerts, c.1600. (By courtesy of the Marquess of Salisbury)

The extraordinary 'Rainbow' portrait of the Queen at Hatfield House (*92*) depicts her wearing a richly embroidered bodice, an orange mantle painted with eyes and ears that passes over her left shoulder, loose hair and a headdress that has been copied from an engraving of a Thessalonian bride in Boissard's *Habitus Variarum Orbis Gentium.* Her left sleeve has been embroidered

93. Unknown lady. Attr. Marcus Gheeraerts, 1590–1600. (Reproduced by gracious permission of Her Majesty the Queen)

with a pearl-studded serpent with a heart hanging from its mouth, symbols of wisdom and the passions respectively. Sir Roy Strong in his book *The Cult of Elizabeth* suggests that Elizabeth is here shown as Astraea, 'Queen of Beauty, whose return to earth brings the flower-decked springtime of the Golden Age',[17] a springtime that is alluded to by the choice of flowers embroidered on her bodice. The rainbow, held in the Queen's hand, symbolizes the peace and prosperity that she has brought to the country after a period of storm. The absence of a farthingale and the combination of loose hair, exotic headdress, embroidered bodice and distinctive mantle suggest that the Queen is wearing masque dress. It is possible that the Queen had taken part in or watched a masque in which this particular theme was enacted. Another possibility is that the complex iconography involved in this portrait would not have worked if normal fashionable dress was worn, and so an unusual and dramatic costume and setting were invented.

At Hampton Court Palace there is a mysterious painting of an unknown lady which has been attributed to Gheeraerts on the grounds of strong stylistic and calligraphic evidence, and has been dated between 1590 and 1600 (*93*). The identity of the lady has been a matter of dispute, with Queen Elizabeth, Arabella Stuart and Frances Vavasour, wife of Sir Thomas Shirley, as the main contenders. The lady wears a white, loose, ankle-length gown which is pulled across the body. It is embroidered with a circling design that encloses roses, birds, fruit, honeysuckle, grapes and a bird with outstretched wings above a gold zigzag motif (possibly a phoenix rising from the ashes). Placed over the left shoulder and draped across the gown to fall in silver fringed diaphanous folds (much of this area has been obliterated) is a silver gauze overgown covered in spangles. The V-neckline of the embroidered gown has a turned-back lace collar, as have the cuffs. A thin black cord is worn round the neck, from which are suspended two rings. White and blue slippers criss-crossed with blue pearls are clearly visible with the shorter hem length. The headdress has been copied from an illustration of a Persian lady in Boissard's *Habitus Variarum Orbis Gentium* (*94*); it is a conical structure covered with gauze and scattered with pansies, with a streamer attached to its top point flowing out behind the lady's loose hair. Pansies also form a garland which the lady is placing on the stag which stands next to her. The unusual and dramatic setting for this painting, the melancholic nature of the verses in the cartouche, the Latin verses in the tree and the extraordinary costume suggest that this is a portrait of a lady in masque dress. If that is the case, setting and costume would be related to the device of the masque in which she was a participant.

Prior to Inigo Jones' designs, there is little visual evidence as to the appearance of male masquers; there are, however, brief descriptions of their costumes in the Revels Accounts. The season of 1573/4, for example, included a masque of lance knights in blue satin with torchbearers in black and yellow satin, and on New Year's Day one with foresters in green satin with cloaks of crimson sarcenet.[18] A painting that was at one time owned by Worthing Museum (unfortunately destroyed during the last war) depicted an Elizabethan man apparently wearing masque costume (*95*). A surviving photograph of the painting shows a three-quarter-length figure clad in a skin-tight black garment which covers all his body

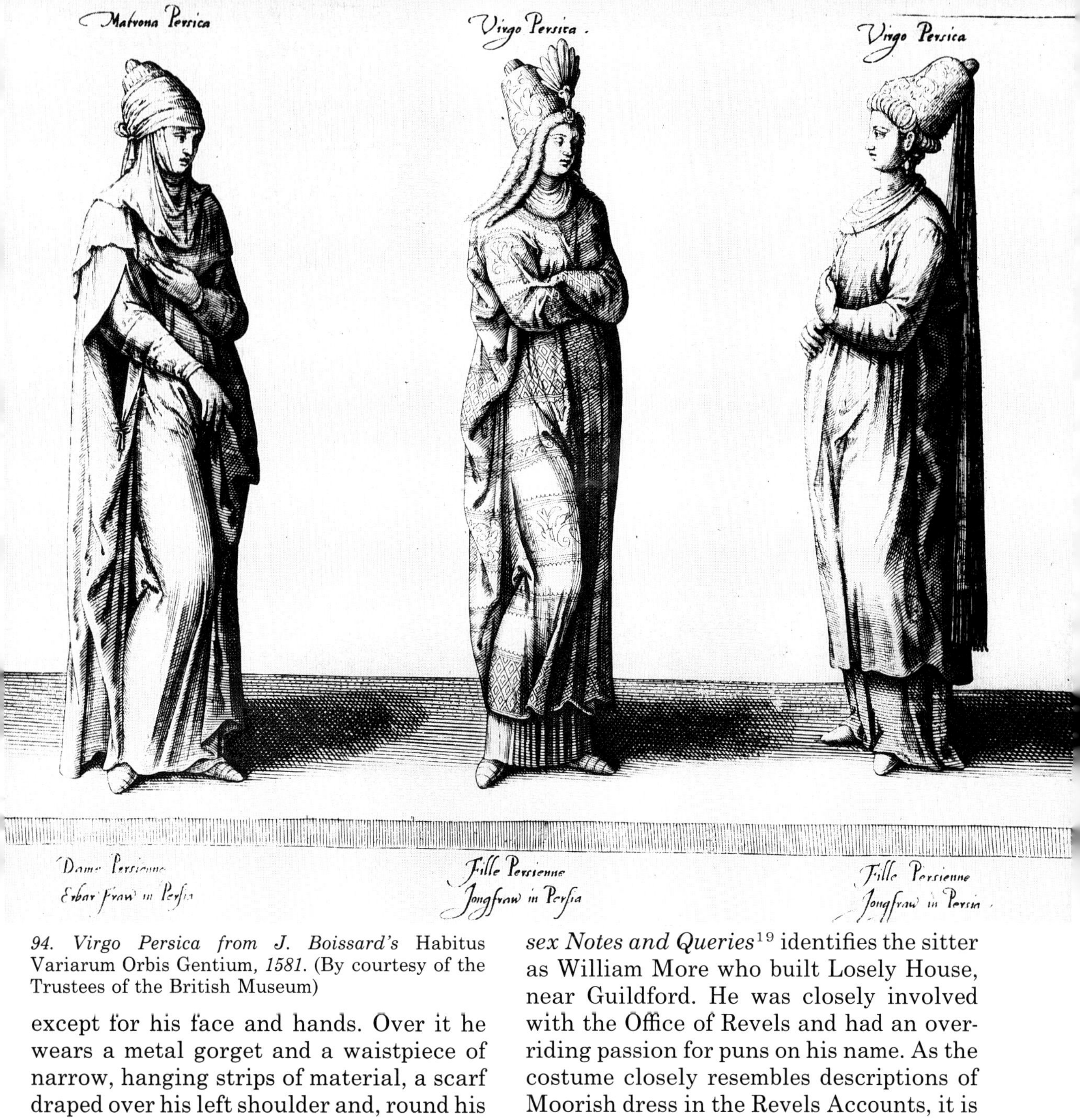

94. Virgo Persica from J. Boissard's Habitus Variarum Orbis Gentium, *1581.* (By courtesy of the Trustees of the British Museum)

except for his face and hands. Over it he wears a metal gorget and a waistpiece of narrow, hanging strips of material, a scarf draped over his left shoulder and, round his neck, a closed ruff. This last item would not seem incongrous, as anachronism in theatrical dress was quite usual. A pearl bracelet encircles one wrist and in the other he clasps a pasteboard shield painted with satyrs and fleeing stags. An article in *Sussex Notes and Queries*[19] identifies the sitter as William More who built Losely House, near Guildford. He was closely involved with the Office of Revels and had an overriding passion for puns on his name. As the costume closely resembles descriptions of Moorish dress in the Revels Accounts, it is perhaps not too fanciful to suggest that he chose to dress up as a Moor for his portrait:

> Each in his plumes, his colours and device,
> Expressing warrior's wit and courtier's grace.[20]

November 17 was Queen Elizabeth's Accession Day, and it was duly celebrated each year by a spectacular tilt at Whitehall Palace. This annual event had become an established feature of court life, possibly as early as 1570, and certainly by 1581. Sir Henry Lee (*88*) organized the events and appeared as the challenger every year, for which activity he was designated Knight of the Crown, a post he held until his retirement in 1590. In the Tilt of 1584 Lee's opponent was Sir Philip Sidney. Sidney was an enthusiastic tilter and deviser of imprese, and it is thought that the description of a tilt in *Arcadia*, Book II, is an account of that very occasion. The description of costumes worn by other knights in *Arcadia* are fascinating; the one worn by the Knight of the Tomb is especially macabre and one wonders whether he existed only in Sidney's imagination or actually appeared in a tournament. The costume uses painting and embroidery to create a bizarre *trompe l'oeil* effect:

> armour, all painted over with such a cunning shadow, that it represented a gaping sepulchre, the furniture of his horse was all of cypresse braunches . . . his bases (which he ware so long, as they came almost to his ankle) were imbrodered onely with blacke wormes, which seemed to crawle up and downe, as readie to devoure him.

Francis Bacon in his essay *Of Masques and Triumphs* summarized the essential ingredients for a successful appearance: 'For justs, and tourneys, and barriers; the glories of them are chiefly in the chariots, wherein the challengers make their entry; especially if they be drawn with strange beasts, as lions, bears, camels and the like; or in the devices of their entrance; or in the bravery of their liveries; or in the godly furniture of their horses and armour.'

95. William More (?). Unknown artist, 1565–70. (Destroyed in the war)

Lee's retirement Tilt of 1590 is well documented, and portraits of two principal participants, the Earl of Essex (colour pl. 7) and the Earl of Cumberland (*96*), have survived. George Peele's poem *Polyhymnia*, 1590, describes in enthusiastic detail the costumes of the knights who took part. Sir Henry's costume took as its theme his retirement and so was embroidered with a 'wither'd running vine'.

In contrast to Lee, Cumberland wore white with 'plumes and pendants as white as swan'; the portrait shows him in the act of challenging, with his gauntlet thrown on to the ground. His blue armour is studded with gold stars, and over it is worn a surcoat of paler blue decorated with bands of gold and jewels. The sleeves are turned back to disclose a white satin lining embroidered with celestial spheres and branches of olive, and this pattern is repeated on the brim of his bonnet. This bonnet would be removed for the actual tilting, when he would wear the helmet that lies on the ground. Colour combinations worn by other knights included ivory and crimson, white and green, silver and sable, but the most sensational costume was worn by the Earl of Essex. He had upset the Queen by marrying without her consent and in order to show his grief he and his entourage wore black, the funereal colour. His portrait by Segar (colour pl. 7) records his dramatic appearance:

> . . . all in sable sad,
> Drawn on with coal-black steeds of dusky hue,
> In stately chariot full of deep device.

Over his plain black armour and white collar Essex wears a black surcoat with narrow hanging sleeves, the entire surface of which is encrusted with a complex trail-

Hasta

96. George Clifford, 3rd Earl of Cumberland. Nicholas Hilliard, c.1590. (The National Maritime Museum, Greenwich)

ing pattern of pearls of different sizes.

Full armour had to be worn for tilting as it was a dangerous, even potentially lethal exercise. The tilt took place in a tilt-yard in the centre of which was a barrier, and the horsemen equipped with long lances raced down either side to meet in the middle with a clash of weapons. Chest armour, whether worn for normal military purposes or on festive occasions, usually echoed the lines of the doublet. That worn by Sir Antony Mildmay, painted by Hilliard in 1595 (*97*), has a pronounced peascod shape and is

97. Sir Anthony Mildmay. Nicholas Hilliard, 1595. (The Cleveland Museum of Art, purchase from the J.H. Wade Fund)

decorated with engraved bands of gilded arabesques.

One of the most impressive sights at the court of Queen Elizabeth in its closing years was the glittering white, gold and silver costume worn by the Maids of Honour. This costume revived certain medieval features, sharp spiky lines and a cluster of filigree decoration, combined with the contemporary taste for pearl-encrusted embroidery and an ostentatious display of jewels. Fortunately, there are several portraits of ladies wearing this costume, and they share several striking features: open, fan-shaped ruffs, serrated hanging sleeves, a flounced farthingale skirt and a distinctive headdress composed of silver, fern-like wires, spangles and pearls.

One of the most beautiful girls at Court was Mary Fitton. She became a Maid of Honour at the age of 16 in 1595 and her portrait was painted by George Gower the following year.[22] The portrait, at Arbury Hall, shows her wearing a magnificent costume comprising a matching stomacher and sleeves which have been decorated with an elaborate latticework pattern composed of vertical and horizontal slashes with serrated borders intersected with a pansy-flower shape, the centre of which is defined by a clump of spangles. Massive hanging sleeves have been cut into sharp peaks, each one finished with a spray of wired spangles. Spangles on wires, called 'hanginge spangles' in the Wardrobe Accounts, were ordered in large amounts to decorate the Maids of Honour clothes in the 1590s; sixty ounces were ordered for a stomacher and sleeves alone for Elizabeth and Ann Russell in 1598.[23] Later in the same year there is a warrant to John Parr, the embroiderer, to decorate a pair of hanging sleeves and wings of white striped satin in a way that is very similar to that worn by Mary and Lady Elizabeth Southwell (*96*). The irregular shiny surface of the satin was to be enhanced by 'silver pynched plate' and the silver tufts were to have hanging spangles 'set in the myddest'. The allowance for this decoration was eight ounces of spangles and five ounces of plate.[24]

A portrait now in the Weiss Gallery, London, of an unknown lady bears such a striking resemblance to Mary Fitton that it is likely that it is a variant of the original portrait (colour pl. 4). Whatever the woman's identity, her elevated social status is indicated by her extraordinarily rich costume and the quantity of elaborate jewels. The white satin stomacher and sleeves have a raised leaf-like pattern studded with pearls, with the space between filled with tiny pearl insects. Grandoise, serrated hanging sleeves outlined with wired peaks and surmounted with spangles rest on the horizontal edge of the flounced farthingale skirt. The preference for square-cut gems in elongated star-shaped settings that first appeared in the early 1590s is well demonstrated by the ruby and black enamel pendants pinned to this lady's sleeve and bodice. Her headdress is constructed out of wired gauze and is decorated with pearls, spangles and jewels. In contrast to the white satin bodice and sleeves studded with pearls, the pearl embroidery on the flounced skirt follows the line of a strong black coiling pattern of leaves.

Mary Fitton's career at Court was short-lived. She became pregnant by William Herbert, Earl of Pembroke, in 1601, and when he refused to marry her she was compelled to return to her family home in

98. Lady Elizabeth Southwell. Marcus Gheeraerts, c.1599. (By kind permission of the Viscount Cowdray)

99. Catherine Killigrew. English school, c.1600. (Ipswich Museum and Art Gallery)

disgrace. Before that sad event she was one of six Maids of Honour who appeared in a masque performed before the Queen in 1600. Lady Elizabeth Southwell also took part, and a full-length portrait of her in her court costume now hangs at Cowdray Park (*98*). Elizabeth was the daughter of Sir Robert Southwell and Lady Elizabeth Howard and was sent to court in December 1599 to become a Maid of Honour. The only surface decoration on her costume of white satin are clusters of pearls on wire stems set in oval compartments, and these also appear on the sleeves and stomacher. Hanging sleeves fall behind, their outer edges serrated and stiffened with wire so that they can carry projecting ornaments of pearls in groups of three. A delicate headdress of silver fern-like leaves embellished with pearls and diamonds decorates her upswept hair. Softening the hard line made by the farthingale is a flounce with radiating pleats.

Ipswich Museum and Art Gallery own a portrait of a wistful-looking lady whose costume is closely related to that worn by Mary and Elizabeth (*99*). The provenance of the painting suggests that it might be a portrait of Catherine Killigrew, daughter of Sir Henry Killigrew, a Groom of the Privy Chamber. The unknown artist has carefully indicated the metallic sheen of her black sleeves, serrated hanging sleeves, bodice and flounced farthingale skirt. Although white was worn by all the court on formal occasions, we know from references in the Wardrobe Accounts that the Queen frequently gave the Maids coloured gowns. This lady's white satin stomacher is enlivened with pearl-encrusted puffs and attached to it is a miniature with a pearl drop. Her open lace ruff is worn with transparent gauze ruching and this material has also been used as a base for the headdress.

The 'straunge fantastick habit' worn by these ladies is the only visual record we have of the elaborate entertainments enacted at the court of Elizabeth I, but a woodcut of a reception given by the Earl of Hertford when the Queen visited him at Elvetham in 1591 affords another glimpse into this charmed and fantastic world (*100*). A large artificial lake was created in the shape of the crescent moon (a reference to Diana, goddess of chastity and by implication the Queen herself), and at its centre was an artificial mount in the shape of a snail. On the water and island various groups of people disguised as sea divinities, Tritons and Virgins waged battle amidst a display of fireworks. The visit lasted a week with an event taking place each day, for which all the participants were suitably attired. On one day the Queen was met by six girls disguised as the three Graces and the three Hours wearing 'Gowns of taffeta sarcenet of divers colours with flourie garlands on their heads and baskets full of sweete herbs and flowers'.[25] Whenever the Queen went on progress throughout the country she would be met by her host's family and retainers disguised as goddesses, shepherds and wild men. They would make speeches of welcome, serenade her with music, act in short plays and offer her gifts. The contrast between the enthusiasm and unsophistication of these displays enacted in the countryside with the artifice of London court life must have further added to their charm.

The costume worn by the Knights, the Maids of Honour, the court masquers and the Queen herself were intended to be

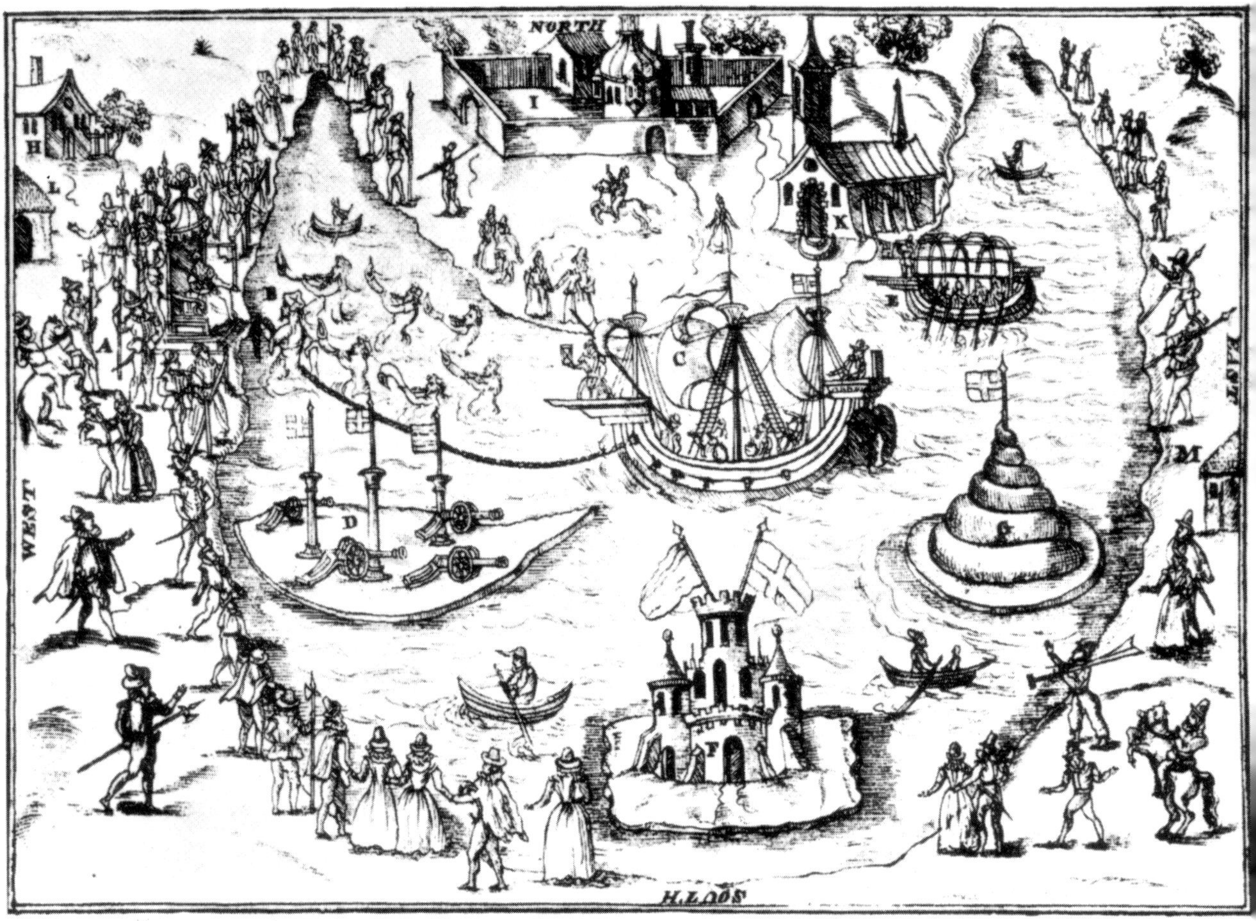

100. Queen Elizabeth I's visit to Elvetham in 1591. Elizabeth can be seen enthroned on the left.

fantastic, for they were worn in an enclosed, highly privileged environment and their very strangeness distanced the wearer from the everyday world and conventional dress. Foreign visitors were always impressed by the display of wealth that these costumes represented but somewhat puzzled by the English preference for the bizarre and the outrageous. Their predilection for distorted shapes and intricately patterned surfaces was also a characteristic of painting, architecture and the decorative arts; whether it be the use of a strong coiling pattern in embroidery or the dramatic silhouette of Hardwick Hall, emphasis was all-important.

The 'inestimable' wardrobe of Queen Elizabeth I represented the highest achievement of Elizabethan embroidery and female fashion. Indeed, it was so impressive that the Italian ambassador wrote in 1603 after the death of Elizabeth that although the new Queen 'declared that she would never wear cast (second-hand) clothes, still it was found that art could not devise anything more costly and gorgeous and so the court dressmakers are at work altering these old robes for nothing new could surpass them.'[25] It was a golden time for English embroidery; the embroiderer's keenly observant eye for the shape of flowers, plants, birds and animals and inventive attitude towards design produced spectacular results. The embroiderer's accuracy in reproducing the natural world in linen and silk was praised by many contemporaries. Shakespeare wrote of the embroideress who:

> . . . with her neeld composes
> Nature's own shape of bud, bird, branch or berry
> That even her art sisters the natural roses:
> Her inkle, silk, twin with the rubied cherry.
> (*Pericles* V, Chorus).

In those examples which have retained their freshness of colour we can fully appreciate this praise and perhaps glimpse the vitality and exuberance that was such an essential feature of Elizabethan dress.

Notes

INTRODUCTION

1 R. Verstegen, *Antiquities concerning the English nation*, 1605
2 *George Vertue Notebooks* IV, *Walpole Society*, 1935–36, page 77. The Reverend John Strype to Ralph Thoresby, 7 October 1708
3 Roy Strong, *Portraits of Queen Elizabeth I*, Oxford University Press, 1963, page 34
4 Foley, *Records of the English Province of the Society of Jesus*, Vol. 1, page 8
5 Quoted in R. Strong, J. Trevelyan Oman, *Elizabeth R*, Secker and Warburg, 1971, page 7
6 Victor Von Klarwill, *Queen Elizabeth and some foreigners*, Bodley Head, 1928, page 376
7 Thomas Nashe, *Christ's Tears over Jerusalem*, 1593. *The works of Thomas Nashe*, ed. R.B. McKerrow, Blackwell, Oxford, 5 vols., 1966, Vol. 2, page 151
8 Roy Strong, *The English Icon*, Routledge and Kegan Paul, 1969, page 49
9 Anon., *Philaster*, V.i.557
10 Sir Henry Wooton, *The Elements of Architecture*, 1624, facsimile edition, Gregg International Publishers Ltd 1969, page 110
11 *The Elizabethan Home discovered in two dialogues by Claudius Hollyband and Peter Erondell*, ed. Muriel St Clare Byren, Methuen 1949

Chapter 1

1 Horace Walpole, *Anecdotes of English Painting*, ed. R.N. Wornum, London, 1862, i, 150
2 William Rye, *England as seen by foreigners in the days of Elizabeth I and James I*, 1865, page 7
3 Quoted in M. Channing Linthicum, *Costume in the drama of Shakespeare and his contemporaries*, Oxford, 1936, page 180
4 New Year's Day Gift List, 1578/9, in John Nichols, *The Progresses and Public Processions of Queen Elizabeth I*, 1823, Vol. 2, pages 251–63
5 John Grange, *Granges Garden, The paynting of a curtizan*, 1577
6 Ben Jonson, *Every Man in his Humour*, III.iii.47
7 John Grange, *op. cit.*
8 Hollyband, Erondell, *op. cit.*, page 39
9 T. Tomkis, *Lingua, Dodsley's Old Plays*, Vol. IX, 1876, page 426
10 Hollyband, Erondell, *op. cit.*, pages 36–40
11 Grange, *op. cit.*
12 William Stubbes, *Anatomny of Abuses in England in 1583*, ed. F.J. Furnivall for *New Shakespeare Society*, 1882, 2 vols., Vol. 1, page 78
13 *Preview, City of York Art Gallery Quarterly*, Vol. XXI, 1968, pages 747–9
14 Stephen Gosson, *Pleasant Quippes for Upstart Newfangled Gentlewoman*, 1596
15 George More, *A true discourse concerning the certain possession and dispossession of seven persons in one family in Lancashire*, 1600. Quoted in G.B. Harrison, *A second Elizabethan Journal, 1595–8*, Routledge, 1938, pages 177–8
16 A.L. Rowse, *Raleigh and the Throckmortons*, Macmillan, 1962, page 114
17 Gosson, *op. cit.*

18 Francis Bacon, 'Of Beauty', *Francis Bacon's Essays*, Everyman's Library, 1966, no. XLIII, page 129

Chapter 2

1 F. Davison, *A poetical rhapsody* ed. H.E. Rollins, Harvard University Press, 1931–2, i, 236
2 Lawrence Stone, 'The anatomny of the Elizabethan aristocracy', *Economic History Review*, Vol. XVIII, 1948, page 5
3 J. Black, *The Reign of Elizabeth 1558–1603*, Oxford University Press, 1983, page 272; Sir John Harrington, *Nugae Antiquae*, 1779, Vol. 2
4 Thomas Dekker, *The Guls Horne-book*, 1609, *The Non-dramatic works*, ed. A.B. Grosart, 1884, Vol. 2, page 224
5 Stubbes, *op. cit.*, page 33
6 George Gascoigne, *A delicate diet for daintie-mouthde droonkardes, The complete works of George Gascoigne*, ed. Cunliffe, 1910, Vol. 2, page 466
7 Hollyband, Erondell, *op. cit.*; Eliot, J., *The Parlement of Prattlers* (from *Orthoepia Gallica*, 1593); Florio, J., *His Firste Fruites*, 1578, *His Second Fruites*, 1591
8 *The Household Papers of Henry Percy, 9th Earl of Northumberland, 1564–1632, Royal Historical Society*, 1962, Vol. 93, page 57
9 Stubbes, *op. cit.*, page 53
10 Bishop Hall, *Virgidemiarum*, 1597/8, Lib. 3, satire 3
11 Stubbes, *op. cit.*, page 51
12 *Much Ado about Nothing*, II.iii.16
13 Stubbes, *op. cit.*, page 55
14 *H.M.C., The Earl of Rutland*, Vol. 4, 1904, December 1598 – December 1599, page 415
15 N. Zwager, *Glimpses of Ben Jonson's London*, Swets and Zeitlinger, 1926, page 106
16 Florio, J., *op. cit.*
17 Stubbes, *op. cit.*, page 61
18 *ibid.*, page 56
19 *ibid.*, page 60
20 *Middlesex County Records*, ed. J. Cordy Jeaffreson, 1886, Vol. 1, 26 April 1584
21 T.S. Willan, *Studies in Elizabethan foreign trade*, Manchester University Press, 1959, page 113
22 *H.M.C. De L'Isle and Dudley Ms. at Penshurst*, 1925, Vol. 2, 1 December 1595
23 Stubbes, *op. cit.*, page 57
24 *Calendar of State Papers, Venetian 1557–8*, Appendix, no. 171, Annibale Litolfi to Guglielmo Gonzaga, Duke of Mantua
25 Bishop Hall, *op. cit.*, Lib. 4, sature 4
26 Rye, *op. cit.*, page 13
27 *Much Ado about Nothing*, III.i.176–8
28 *Inventory of the effects of Henry Howard, Earl of Northampton, 1614. Archaeologia*, Vol. XLII, 1869, page 367

Chapter 3

1 Thomas Platter, *Travels in England, 1599*, trans. C. Williams, 1937, page 156
2 Quoted in Rye, *op. cit.*, page 69
3 John Lyly, *Midas, The Prologue in Paul's*, 1592, *The complete works*, Clarendon Press, 1925, ed. R.W. Bond, Vol. III, pages 113–64
4 W. Sanderson, *Aulicus Coquinariae*, 1650, quoted in B. White, *Cast of Ravens*, John Murray, page 122
5 John Gage, *The History and Antiquities of Hengrave*, London, 1822, pages 213–14
6 Roy Strong, *The English Icon*, plate 126
7 Shrewsbury tradesman's invoice, *Shropshire Archaeological and Natural History Society Transactions*, Vol. 2, 1879, page 400
8 Earl of Leicester to Thomas Baroncelli, *H.M.C. Report on the Pepys Ms. Magdalene College, Cambridge*, 1911, page 46
9 *Letters of Philip Gawdy*, Ms. Egerton 2804, British Museum, f.62, f.41, f.90. Ed. I.H. Jeayes, no. 148 Roxburghe Club, London, 1906
10 J. Eliot, *op. cit.*, dialogue 6
11 Nashe, *op. cit.*
12 Hollyband and Erandell, *op. cit.* page 61
13 John Stow, *The Annales or generall Chronicle of England . . . continued and augmented by Edmond Howes, 1615*, page 1039
14 *Henry IV Part 1*, I.iii.35
15 Thomas Middleton, *A Chaste Maid in Cheapside*, I.ii.31, *The works of Thomas Middleton*, ed. A.H. Bullen, John C. Nimmo, London, 1885–6
16 Margaret Hoby, *Diary of an English gentlewoman, Royal Historical Society, 3rd series*, Vol. 2, 1908, page 160

17 Nicholas Breton, 'The Fort of Fancy' from *A Floorish upon Fancy*, 1577, *The Works in Verse and Prose*, Chertsey Worthies 'Library, ed. A.B. Grosart, 1879
18 Thomas Heywood, T., *The Fayre Mayde of the Exchange*, 1607, *The Dramatic Works of Thomas Heywood*, ed. R.H. Shepherd, John Pearson, 1874, Vol. 2, page 42
19 Rutland, *op. cit.*, Vol. 4, page 412
20 IV.vi.79
21 *H.M.C. Seymour Papers at Longleat*, Vol. 4, 4 November 1603, page 164
22 Stow, John, *A Survey of London*, ed. from 1603 edition by C.L. Kingsford, 1908, Vol. 1, page 345
23 Rutland, *op. cit.*, Vol. 4, page 388
24 Gage, *op. cit.*, pages 213–14
25 Overbury, *op. cit.*, page 59
26 De L'Isle, Vol. 1, page 263
27 Overbury, *op. cit.*, page 66
28 Thomas Middleton, *The Black Book*, 1604, *op. cit.*, Vol. 8, page 29
29 *The meeting of gallants at an ordinarie or in the walkes in Powles*. Ed. J. Halliwell, *Percy Society*, London, 1841, Vol. 5, page 10
30 *Sir Giles Goosecap*, II.i.979, Tudor Facsimile Texts, 1912
31 *Inventory of James Backhouse*, 1578, *Surtees Society*, 1853, page 275
32 De L'Isle, *op. cit.*, Vol. 2, page 327

Chapter 4

1 Sir Philip Sidney, *Defence of Poesie*, 1595, *The complete works of Philip Sidney*, ed. Albert Feuillerat, Cambridge 1912–26, Vol. 3, page 9
2 John Mayne, *City Match*, II.ii.227, *Dodsley's Old Plays*, Vol. 13
3 Rosemary Freeman, *English Emblem books*, Chatto and Windus, 1948, page 99
4 John Nevinson, *Embroidery patterns of Thomas Trevelyon, Walpole Society*, Vol. 41, 1966–8
5 L.21/2 f.44r. Public Record Office, Inventory of the Queen's Wardrobe taken in 1599
6 Stowe 557 f.46r, no.4, Manuscript Room, British Museum, Inventory taken in 1600 of the contents of the Queen's Wardrobe
7 *ibid.* f. 50v, no.56
8 *ibid.* f.60r, no.61
9 *ibid.* f.61r, no.70
10 *ibid.* f.50v, no.51
11 *ibid.* f.50v, no.53
12 Stowe 774, 20 November 1580
13 Stowe 557 f.50r, no.59
14 Von Klarwill, *op. cit.*, page 394
15 Nichols, *op. cit.*, Vol. 3, page 134. Also '*Speeches delivered to her Maiestie this last progress at . . . Bisham*', 1592, British Library
16 George Peele, *Speeches to Queen Elizabeth at Theobald's*, *The works of George Peele*, ed. A.H. Bullen, 1888, Vol. 2, page 310. There is a glass painting at Losely House of a basket of lilies, roses and eglantine that is inscribed with the royal mottoes, *Rosa Electa, Foelicior Phoenice*
17 Stowe 557 f.49v
18 New Year's Day Gift List, 1584, transcribed by John Nevinson and published in *Costume*, the Journal of the Costume Society, no. 9, 1975, pages 27–31
19 *H.M.C. Report on the ms. of A.G. Finch*, 1913, Vol. 1, page 25
20 Quoted in Linthicum, *op. cit.*, pages 13–52
21 Thomas Whythorne, *The Autobiography of Thomas Whythorne*, ed. J. Osborn, Oxford University Press, 1962, page 40
22 *Calendar of State Papers, Spanish 1558–1567*, Guzman de Silva to the King of Spain 10 July 1564, letter no. 256
23 Leslie Hotson, *The First Night of Twelfth Night*, Hart-Davies, 1964, page 198
24 *Percy Society*, London, 1845, Vol. 15, page 11
25 Ben Jonson, *Every Man in his Humour*, III.iii.80–84
26 Ben Jonson, *Cynthia's Revels*, II.iii.62–4
27 *The Diary of Ann Clifford*, ed. Vita Sackville-West, 1923, page 42
28 Thomas Nashe, *Summer's Last Will and Testament*, 1600, *Dodsley's Old Plays*, Vol. 8, page 24
29 Catalogue number T.378–1976, dated *c*.1600, so motif current before Peacham
30 Stowe 557 f.31v, no.11
31 Play published in *Materialen zur kunde des alteren Englischen dramas*, 1912, edited by Albert Feuillerat, lines 362–9
32 Astrophel and Stella LIV, *Silver Poets of the Sixteenth Century*, ed. G. Bullett, Dent, 1967, page 193

33 Samuel Daniel, *The worthy tract of Paulus Iouius, contayning a Discourse of rare intentions both Militarie and Amorous called Imprese*, 1585. *The complete works of Samuel Daniel*, ed. A.B. Grosart, 1896, Vol. 4, pages 1–27
34 Daniel Bartoli, quoted in Mark Girouard, *Robert Smythson and the architecture of the Elizabethan era*, Country Life Ltd, 1966, page 40. Reprinted and revised by Yale University Press, 1983

Chapter 5

1 *Tudor Royal Proclamations, Vol. 2, The Later Tudors*, ed. P.L. Hughes and J.F. Larkin, Yale University Press, 1969
2 Stubbes, *op. cit.*, page 34
3 *ibid.*
4 A.L. Rowse, *The England of Elizabeth: the structure of society*, Macmillan, 1950, page 248
5 *Tudor Royal Proclamations*, *op. cit*, no.542, pages 278–83
6 F. Emmison, *Elizabeth Life: Disorder*, Essex County Council, 1970, page 30
7 *The epigrams of John Harrington*, ed. N.E. McClure, 1926, page 207, no.364
8 *Tudor Proclamations*, *op. cit.*, page 189
9 *ibid.*, page 190
10 *ibid.*, page 191
11 Linthicum, *op. cit.*, page 227. See also John Nevinson, *The Dress of the citizens of London 1540–1640, Collectaea Londiniensia, London and Middlesex Archaeological Society*, 1978, pages 265–80
12 J. Stow, *Annales*, pages 1039–40
13 Overbury, *op. cit.*, page 45
14 Linthicum, *op. cit.*, page 27, note 3
15 William Harrison, *A description of England in 1578*, ed. F.J. Furnivall, 1889, page 197
16 Stow, *op. cit.*, page 89
17 Rutland, *op. cit.*, Vol. 4, page 486
18 *The Diary of John Dee, Camden Society, Old Series 19*, 1842, page 54
19 Stowe 774, *Accompt Book of Roger North, 2nd Baron North of Kirtling 1575–81, 1582–9*, British Museum. Part published in *Archaeologia*, Vol. XIX, 1821, pages 283–301
20 Gawdy, *op. cit.*, f.129
21 Von Klarwill, *op. cit.*, page 326
22 *Calendar State Papers, Domestic, 1597*, page 492
23 Stowe 142, no.23, 13 November 1603. Quoted in E.K. Chambers, *The English Stage*, Oxford, 1923, Vol. 1, page 40
24 L/C 5/37, *Public Record Office Wardrobe Warrant Book*, 1598, p. 129
25 Further information in J.H. Baker's 'A history of Judges' Robes', in *Costume*, the Journal of the Costume Society, 1978, no.12, pages 27–39
26 Robert Greene, *A Notable Discovery of Coosnage now daily practised by sundry lewd persons, called Connie-biters*, Bodley Head Quarto, 1923, page 186
27 Francis Thynne, *The Debate between Pride and Lowliness*, 1570, *The Shakespeare Society*, London, 1841, pages 9–10
28 *ibid.*, page 33
29 Platter, *op. cit.*, pages 182–3
30 M.L. Campbell, *The English Yeoman under Elizabeth and the early Stuarts*, Merlin Press, 1967, page 253
31 Platter, *op. cit.*, page 177. Also *Calendar State Papers Venetian 1617–19*, page 61
32 Von Klarwill, *op. cit.*, page 326
33 *ibid.*, page 377
34 A.L. Rowse, *Simon Forman: Sex and Society in Shakespeare's Age*, Macmillan, 1974, page 93
35 Campbell, *op. cit.*, page 253

Chapter 6

1 Nashe, *op. cit.*, Vol. 2, page 142
2 Bacon, *op. cit.*, Essay no.XXXVII, page 115
3 Francis Yates, 'Boissard's costume book and two portraits', *Journal of the Warburg and Courtauld Institute*, 1959, pages 373–4. *See also*, J. Olian, *Sixteenth Century Costume Books, Dress*, Vol. 3, 1977, pages 20–48
4 Edward Hall, *The Union of the two noble and illustre families of Lancaster and York*, 1809 edn, ed. Sir H. Ellis, 1809, page 526
5 Chambers, *op. cit.*, Vol. 1, page 72
6 F. Boas, *Queen Elizabeth in drama and related studies*, Allen and Unwin, 1950, page 48
7 Chambers, *op. cit.*, page 16
8 Bacon, *op. cit.*, page 116
9 Albert Feuillerat, 'Office of the Revels in the time of Queen Elizabeth', published in *Materialen zu Kunde des alteren Englischen Dramas*, 1908, page 180

10 *ibid.*, pages 286–7
11 Roy Strong, *The cult of Elizabeth*, Thames and Hudson, 1977: III 'Sir Henry Unton and his portrait', pages 84–110
12 Feuillerat, *op. cit.*, page 208. Masks were also worn during the day to protect the complexion
13 Stella Mary Newton, *Renaissance Theatre Costume*, 1975, page 213
14 Philip Sidney, *The Countess of Pembroke's Arcadia*, Vol. 1, pages 75–6
15 John Nichols, *op. cit.*, Vol. 3, page 364
16 De L'Isle, *op. cit.*, Vol. 2, page 468, 14 June 1600
17 Strong, *Cult of Elizabeth*: Part one: 1 'The Queen: *Eliza Triumphans*', pages 50–54
18 Feuillerat, *op. cit.*, pages 189–221
19 L.F. Salzmann, 'A sixteenth century portrait', *Sussex Notes and Queries* Vol. 8, 1941
20 George Peele, *Polyhymnia*, 1590, *The Works of George Peele*, ed. A.H. Bullen, 1888, Vol. 2, pages 287–302
21 *Arcadia*, Lib 3, ch. 16, Vol. 1, page 445
22 Portrait reproduced in Strong, *The English Icon* no.146
23 L.C.5/37, page 130, Public Record Office
24 John Lyly, *Entertainments at Elvetham*, 1591, Vol. 1, page 439
25 *Calendar of State Papers, Venetian 1603–7*, 10 July 1603, letter no.91

Glossary

Aglets ornamental metal tags that could either be attached to points or used in pairs with no visible tie and so could be used as a fastening or as a purely decorative trimming

Apron a linen or wool apron with or without a bib would be worn by the working classes and by country housewives. Aprons without a bib and made of the finest material were worn by the fashionable lady at home towards the end of the century

Band collar of linen worn about the neck of a shirt or smock

Bandstrings the tasselled ties that were threaded through the collar in order to fasten it

Bases lower skirt-like part of tunic worn over armour

Beaver the silky fur of the beaver was used for the expensive and fashionable hat called a beaver

Billiment (also *billament*) a decorative border, often made of gold and studded with jewels, that was used to edge the upper curve of a French hood and the lower (or *nether*) curve. Also worn separately as a hair ornament

Blackwork black silk embroidery on white linen

Bobbin lace a patterned lace made from threads attached to bobbins

Bodyes a bodice was referred to as a 'pair of bodyes', as it was made in two parts joined together at the side

Bombast padding made from cotton, wool or horsehair that was used to produce a stiff, swollen shape

Bongrace the projecting, usually detached, brim of a bonnet, cap or coif used to protect the complexion

Boothose overstocking with richly embroidered top that would be turned down over the boot

Breeches from about 1570 this term denoted an alternative style of legwear to trunk hose. It was worn with separate stockings and covered the area from the waist to the knee. See also *venetians*, *galligaskins*

Busk a strip of wood, whalebone or metal that was inserted in a casing in the bodice in order to stiffen it

Buskin a covering for the foot or leg reaching to the calf or to the knee; when worn in Greek tragedy it was a high thick-soled boot

Busk-point a tie for securing the busk

Camlet a name originally applied to a costly Oriental cloth, afterward to a substitute made from various mixed materials

Canions tubular extension of the hose which closely fitted the leg to below the kneecap
Carcenet heavy necklace of gold and jewels that resembled a collar
Caul hairnet made of gold thread or silk, lined and decorated
Chemise another term for smock; a lady's linen undergarment
Chin-clout large square of material worn over the chin, often seen in pictures of country women
Close-bodied gown gown that was shaped to the waist, from where it fell in folds to the ground
Cloth of gold a material woven with a warp of pure gold threads and weft of silk. Used by royalty and the nobility
Codpiece bag-like appendage, attached by points to the hose, that concealed the opening in front of the hose
Coif small linen cap which covered the head and was tied under the chin
Colley-Westonward way of wearing a mandilion with one sleeve hanging over the chest, and one at the back
Cony (also *coney*) the fur of a rabbit
Comfit-box a box of sweetmeats
Crippin (also *crepine, crespine*) a crimped or pleated frill
Cutwork needle lace of Italian origin made by cutting out squares from fabric and then filling the spaces with geometric designs. Also called *reticella*
Damask a rich silk made with either a floral or geometric pattern
Doublet close-fitting upper garment worn over the shirt
Drawer one who drew designs on to fabric that would then be embroidered
Dutch cloak a sleeved cloak, usually guarded
Falling band a shirt collar that has been turned down
Farthingale (also fuardingall) an understructure consisting of a series of connected hoops that increased in circumference from the waist to the feet
Forehead cloth a triangular piece of material that was worn with a matching coif
Forepart triangular piece of material that filled in the central parted section of the skirt
French cloak long full cloak generally worn draped over the left shoulder
French farthingale a wheel-shaped structure worn under the skirt so that the skirt would be carried out at right angles before falling vertically to the feet. It was worn with a slight tilt forward, a tilt that became increasingly exaggerated after 1600
French hood a small hood worn far back on the head that consisted of a curved front border and horseshoe-shaped curve on the top of the crown
Frieze a kind of coarse woollen cloth with a nap on one side only
Frizado a woollen cloth similar to frieze but of better quality
Galligaskins full baggy breeches
Gauze transparent woven silk material
Girdle narrow cord, band or chain that followed the waistline. It was usually decorated and, in the case of female dress, used to support a number of items
Gorget a military steel or plate armour collar worn over the chest. When used in the context of female dress it was another word for wimple, the piece of linen that was folded so that it enveloped the head, chin, sides of face and neck
Guard band of material used either as a decorative border or to cover a seam. It was made of a contrasting material and colour to the garment
Hangers support for a sword that was attached to the sword-belt
Hanging sleeve a false decorative sleeve that usually matched the doublet, if worn by a man, or the bodice, if worn by a woman
Hanging spangles sequins attached to wires

Head-rail a square of starched linen arranged around the head; during the later part of the century it was trimmed with lace and spangles and wired into decorative shapes

Hose the covering for a man's body from the waist down. The term 'hose' was usually applied to the upper portion and did not denote stockings until the mid-seventeenth century. Stockings were referred to as *nether stocks* or *nether stockings*

Jacket waist-length garment worn for warmth

Jerkin sleeved or sleeveless fitted garment worn over the doublet

Kendall a coarse woollen cloth, usually green

Kerchief (also *neckerchief*) a large square of material folded lengthways and used as a shawl for the shoulders

Kersey a coarse woollen cloth of variable quality

Kirtle before 1545 this term denoted bodice and skirt but after that date the skirt alone

Linen a material woven from flax that ranged in quality from coarse buckram and dowlas to lawn, a very fine and expensive linen used for ruffs, collars and rails

Loose gown an overgarment that fell in loose folds from the shoulders. Also called an *open gown*

Mandilion loose jacket with a standing collar and hanging sleeves

Mantle if worn on ceremonial occasions, a long garment that was open in front and reached to the ground. Also called a *veil* in inventories, and appears to have been worn like a shawl. When the mantle was worn with masque dress it was draped asymmetrically across the body

Mary Stuart hood a hood that was wired into a heart shape

Mask worn outdoors and in bed to protect the complexion. Also worn at masques to disguise the features

Mercer one who dealt in expensive imported fabrics

Milliner one who sold fancy goods and fashionable accessories

Mules flat backless shoes

Nightcap linen cap, usually embroidered, worn indoors by men

Network lace consisting of a ground of square meshes on which is worked the pattern

Nightgown loose, lined gown worn by men and women either indoors for warmth and comfort or outdoors as an overgarment. Usually lined with fur

Oes small metal rings or eyelets used to decorate the surface of material

Ordinary an eating-house or tavern which provided a meal at a fixed price

Pane method of decorating material, either by slashing the whole length vertically, leaving top and bottom joined, or by applying separate strips of material that are attached top and bottom to the background

Pantofles overshoes with long front uppers and thick cork soles

Partlet decorative accessory that covered the upper part of the chest and was attached to the bodice

Paul's (or *Pawle's*) popular name for St Paul's Cathedral, London, a meeting-place for fashionable gentlemen

Peascod name given to exaggerated style of doublet fashionable in the 1580s and 1590s

Petticoat underskirt

Pinking small holes or slits cut into material and arranged to form a pattern

Pickadil either tabs set at right angles to form a border or, at the end of the century, a wired or stiffened support for a standing band

Points ties with metal tags

Poking-stick (also *setting-stick*) a rod of wood, bone or steel that was heated in order to set the pleats of a ruff

Pomander a perforated container for perfume
Pouncet box a small box with perforated lid for perfume
Puke a woollen textile dyed before weaving, of varying quality
Puffs decorative effect produced when material was drawn out through slashes and panes
Rail square of material folded horizontally and worn on the head or round the shoulders like a shawl
Rebato shaped collar pinned to the bodice and wired so that it stood up round the back of the head
Ruff originally the frill that edged the standing collar of a shirt. Ruffs increased in size until, by the 1570s, they had become separate articles. With the use of starch and setting-sticks, ruffs could be very wide and consist of many layers
Russet coarse woollen homespun material largely used by country people
Sarcenet a thin soft silk textile having a slight sheen on the surface
Shadow (also called a cornet) a limp cap of linen, lawn, cypress, network or lace that encircled the upper half of the forehead
Shag thick-piled cloth often used for linings
Slashing slits of varying length cut in a garment and arranged in a pattern
Spangs sequins
Spanish cloak a full, short cloak with a hood
Spanish farthingale understructure which produced either a funnel-shaped or bell-shaped skirt
Startups loose leather shoes worn by country people that reached above the ankle. Sometimes they would be laced and buckled up, sometimes loose-fitting
Stockings worn by men and women, they could be tailored or knitted and made from a wide variety of materials, silk being the most expensive
Stomacher inverted triangle of stiffened material attached to the front of the bodice
Surcoat loose, usually sleeveless, overgarment
Tuff taffeta a kind of taffeta with a pile or nap arranged in tufts
Trunk hose a style of hose which swelled out from the waistband to turn directly on to the thighs
Underpropper wire frame attached to the collar that supported the ruff pinned to it
Velvet a very popular material that was available in a wide range of colours and could be either plain or figured. Figured velvet was woven in two colours with two and sometimes three piles. Wrought velvet was velvet with an embroidered pattern
Venetians full breeches closed at the knee. They could either be voluminous throughout or close-fitting
Waistcoat informal jacket-style garment worn by men and women
Wing roll of stiffened material that hid the join between sleeve and armhole. It could be decorated in a number of ways

Select bibliography

Arnold, J., *Lost from her Majesties Back: The Day Book of the Wardrobe of Robes. Costume Society Extra Series no.7*

—*Elizabethan and Jacobean smocks and shirts. Waffen und Kostumkunde*, 1973, Vol. XV pp. 109–24

—*The secrets of Queen Elizabeth's Wardrobe unlocked.* W.S. Maney, 1987

Buxton, J., *Elizabethan Taste.* Macmillan, 1963

Byrne, M. St Clare, *The Elizabethan home discovered in two dialogues*, 1949

Chalfont, F.C., *Ben Jonson's London. A London Placename Dictionary*, University of Georgia Press, 1978

Cunnington, C.W. and P., *Handbook of English Costume in the 16th century.* Faber, 1962

Cunnington, P., *Occupational costume in England from the 11th century to 1914.* Black, 1976

Digby, G.W., *Elizabethan embroidery.* Faber, 1963

Feuillerat, A., *Office of the Revels in the time of Queen Elizabeth.* Published in *Materialen zu Kunde des alteren, Englischen Dramas*, 1908

Gawdy, P. *The Letters of Philip Gawdy 1579–1616.* I. Jeayes, *Roxburghe Club* (ed.), London, no. 148, 1906

Harrison, W., *A description of England in 1578.* F. Furnivall (ed.), 1889

Hussey, M., *The world of Shakespeare and his contemporaries.* Heineman, 1971

Linthicum, M.C., *Costume in the drama of Shakespeare and his contemporaries.* Oxford, 1936

Nevinson, J., *Connoisseur*, Vol. XCVII, 1936, pp. 25 and 140. *English embroidered costume*

—Vol. CIII, 1939. Part 1: *Unrecorded types of embroidery in the collection of Lord Middleton.* Part 2: *English embroidered costume in the collection of Lord Middleton*

—*Catalogue of English domestic embroidery of the 16th and 17th centuries.* The Victoria & Albert Museum, 1938

—*Journal of the Costume Society, no.9*, 1975. *New Year's Day Gift List of 1584*

—*Illustrations of costume in the Alba Amicorum. Archaeologia*, Vol. 106, 1979, pp. 167–176

Nichols, J., *The Progresses and Public Processions of Queen Elizabeth I*, 1823

Platter, T., *Thomas Platter's travels in England in 1599.* Clare Williams (trans.), 1937

Rye, W., *England as seen by foreigners in the days of Elizabeth I and James I*, 1865

Seligman, S. and Hughes, T., *Domestic Needlework. Country Life*, 1926

Strong, R., *Portraits of Queen Elizabeth I.* Oxford University Press, 1969

—*The English Icon.* Routledge and Kegan Paul, 1969

—*The Cult of Elizabeth: Elizabethan portraiture and pageantry.* Thames and Hudson, 1977

—*The English Renaissance Miniature.* Thames and Hudson, 1983

—*Gloriana: The Portraits of Queen Elizabeth I.* Thames and Hudson, 1987

Stubbes, P., *Anatomny of Abuses in England in 1583.* F. Furnivall (ed.) for *New Shakespeare Society*, 1882

—*The Diary of Baron Waldstein. A traveller in Elizabethan London.* Translated and annotated by G.W. Groos, Thames and Hudson, 1981

Wilson, J., *Entertainments for Elizabeth I.* Boydell and Brewer, 1980

EXHIBITION CATALOGUES

The Elizabethan Image, Tate Gallery, 1969

Artists of the Tudor Court. The portrait miniature rediscovered 1520–1620. Victoria & Albert Museum, 1983

The Triumphant Image. An exhibition of Tudor and Stuart Portraits. Christchurch Mansion, Ipswich, 1987

Princely Magnificence: Court Jewels of the Renaissance. Victoria & Albert Museum, 1981

Index

Numbers in *italic* type refer to illustrations.